JOURNEY TO THE CENTER OF MY SOUL

A CONVERSATION WITH CHRIST

JOURNEY TO THE CENTER OF MY SOUL

A CONVERSATION WITH CHRIST

DENNIS JOSEPH EUGENE O'DONNELL

LEONINE PUBLISHERS
PHOENIX, ARIZONA

ISBN-13: 978-0-9859483-3-7

Library of Congress Control Number: 2012946668

Printed in the United States of America
10 9 8 7 6 5 4 3 2

Published by Leonine Publishers LLC
Phoenix, Arizona
USA

Visit us online at www.leoninepublishers.com
For more information: info@leoninepublishers.com

Acknowledgments

There are many people who I would like to thank for bringing me closer to God the Father, through His Son, Jesus Christ, and the Holy Spirit.

First I would like to thank my two daughters, Terra and Renee, for always demanding the best I had to offer. They may not realize it, but it's because of them that I maintained the slightest resemblance of a Christian. Because I was so worried about their souls, I may indeed save my own in the process.

Secondly I would like to thank my mother for the use of her conscience which had to work overtime while mine was on the fritz. I thank her for all her prayers which undoubtedly played a major role in my conversion. Mom always believed I was a good person even though I now realize she was perhaps optimistic. I may have been good on the outside, but inside I may as well have been dead. I would also like to thank her for introducing me to Father Corapi and the EWTN network.

I must thank Mother Angelica and the EWTN network for the part they played in my reconversion. Just as Mother Angelica was steering the ship, Father Corapi threw me the life preserver and pulled me to the ship. Although he has since left the priesthood, facts are facts and regardless of current circumstances, John Corapi played a large role in my reconversion. I feel horrible for him and I pray for him as well, but at no time did I ever take my eyes off Christ crucified. Behind me in a raft were Father Groeschel, Raymond Arroyo, and Marcus Grodi to make sure I made it.

Despite all the assistance, no one could help me climb the ladder. All anyone could do was cheer for me and watch—but I had to climb the ladder and get on board. The same is true for whoever reads this book. You can judge this book and perhaps deep down agree with most, if not all of it. I only wrote what I've been told and I made it very clear if I interjected my opinion.

Dear reader, you have to decide you want a real relationship with God the Father, Christ, the Holy Spirit, and the Blessed Mother. You have to make the changes and commitment in your life that will bring about your eternal salvation. Sitting on the sideline will not get you to heaven. Some may say they believe in God but don't see a need for the Church. I say if you truly loved and knew God, you wouldn't want to ever leave the Church.

If you were to tell me that you have a relationship with God outside the Church and He understands where you're coming from, I would have to tell you that you do in fact have a relationship outside the Church. It most likely isn't with God because I myself once had that same relationship.

CONTENTS

INTRODUCTION

This book addresses the relationship between Christ and me. I was asked to write it as a way of sparking interest in my story. Actually, this book is "inspired" and two of the stories were practically dictated to me as I typed. I did not use any last names or the names of any of the companies for which I've worked. In fact, looking back I'm thankful for everything I've been through and for everyone I've interacted with over the years. In every chance encounter, one either gains something or loses something, but we're never the same. Do we always notice it? No, of course we don't. Sometimes we never notice and other times it could be weeks, months, or years before something will jog our memory. We then recall what was said or what happened, and we come away with a deeper understanding. Yes, I'm thankful for everyone in my life. Without each and every one—good and bad—I wouldn't have arrived at this place in my life, which is an unbelievable relationship with my Best Friend, Jesus Christ.

As you read this book, I pray that you see where God was very active in my life. There were several times where God or my guardian angel intervened to save my life. I knew it then but I never understood it. I always wondered what it was about me and why my life had been spared. I often ask myself the question, Why didn't I change my ways back then? The only answer I have is that I was young and invincible. It was literally by the grace of God that none of my escapades cost me my life, for I'm certain it would have meant death with no opportunity for eternal life with my Best Friend, Jesus Christ, His Father, and the Holy Spirit.

In the pages that follow, I briefly describe some of the events I feel emphasize my point of being born for a specific purpose. Throughout my life I always felt I was supposed to do something else. Until now I never knew what it was. I'm certain my initial calling was to be a priest, but I ignored the calling; choosing instead to follow my own path and adhering to my own set of rules. I truly believe—I know—my new purpose in life is to call attention to the Catholic Faith, to deepen the faith of those who are confused, or for lack of a better phrase, those who are fence-sitters. This was probably not God's original plan for me because as I said, I've always felt I was born for another purpose. Through the grace of God I raised two incredible daughters and in the end I responded to the call of God through His Son Jesus Christ.

I was given a second chance at life. Not everyone is as fortunate as I. I will not waste another minute of my life. I now live for God. I prayed and begged God to give me an opportunity to redeem myself. I asked Him for the opportunity to make Him proud of me. He decided to answer my prayers. It is by the grace of God that I'm here today. It is also by the grace of God I'm able to write this book. I sincerely pray that this book can save many people from the turmoil and tribulation of trying to live life without God. Truly, with God all things are possible. Without God nothing is even feasible. I pray those of you who find yourself in the same situation will take my lead and humble yourselves before God. I guarantee you He's waiting with open arms.

At present I drive a truck. I operate under my own authority and own the truck I drive. The truck is equipped with a kitchen, refrigerator, flat screen TV, surround sound, a shower and toilet, and hardwood floors; but in the end it is a truck. I drive it and that makes me a truck driver. I obtained my own authority with the intention of getting my own accounts and building a fleet second to none. I was well-liked and respected in the entertainment business and could obtain all the business I could handle; yet, I desired to do something that would enable me to get home more often. There were several years that I made it home less than ten days a year. Before applying for my authority, I spent months, and I'm sure hundreds of hours, methodically researching the companies I intended to call on. I was studying them backward and forward, checking to see if they had any recurring complaints or damage. I had every intention of making a name for myself and a substantial amount of money as well. I did get my own authority but nothing else went as scripted. My life changed dramatically.

I felt myself getting closer and closer to God during this time, more specifically to Jesus Christ. I was confident that with the help of Christ I couldn't fail. I figured all I had to do was continue to pray the rosary, read the Bible, and lead a clean life. In return, I would be successful, perhaps find the right woman, and make money hand-over-fist. Somewhere between praying the rosary, reading the Bible, and leading a clean life I continued to get closer to Christ.

Gradually I began to give everything up. By "everything" I mean the plans for my business, the hope of ever finding the right woman, and any concerns about money. I quit tobacco and gambling, and I worked really hard at controlling my temper. I became so close to Christ I promised Him I would never remarry or enter into another relationship. Not that a relationship is bad, but I'm not capable of both. I personally do not feel I can serve God to the fullest while at the same time being a husband because I always felt alone. Although I cannot deny that Catholic marriage is a sacrament. In any event, I couldn't bear the pain of losing the relationship I now enjoy with Christ. For the first time in my life, I feel good about myself and what I'm doing.

I now have purpose in my life. I spend the majority of my day in prayer, either through the rosary or my own, reading the Bible, or listening to a CD of the New Testament. I also spend time studying the history of the Catholic Church and studying the New Testament. Add to that listening or watching EWTN. Did I plan this? No, not in a million years did I see this coming. God is now very much in control of my life. My life has changed so much! Everything is opposite of where it was prior to the spiritual experiences. As most everyone else, I prayed and read the Bible when I had the time. Now reading the Bible is a daily exercise, as well as several different forms of prayer throughout the day. I was once so immersed in prayer I paid my bills two weeks late. That's right, I pay all of my bills around the first of the month, but I was so caught up in prayer I completely lost track of time, which resulted in some of my bills being late. Can you imagine me calling and asking company XYZ to waive the late fee because I was praying?

The pages that follow are a very brief description of my life before my reconversion. This book is really about my life and friendship with Christ, as nothing in my prior life really matters (with the exception of my two daughters, mother, family, and a few other people). With the exception of my role as a father, the former Dennis O'Donnell no longer exists.

To understand who I am is to first know who and what I'm not. I'm not a priest, deacon, evangelist, or theologian. I'm not a Biblical scholar or a seminarian. I'm not even a parishioner; I attend Mass wherever I happen to be. I've walked as far as four miles one way, I've taken several cabs, and on one occasion I rented a car. Quite often I'll drop my trailer and drive the truck to Mass if the parking is adequate; however, this is my least favorite option. I am a son, brother, father, cousin, and truck driver. My name is Dennis Joseph Eugene O'Donnell.

My first and last names are self explanatory. Joseph is the name my parents chose for me at the time of my Baptism, Eugene was my grandfather's name; a man I loved very much. Eugene is the name I chose at the time of my Confirmation. My name is Dennis Joseph Eugene O'Donnell, and I am Catholic.

Chapter One

SPARED LIFE

My life has been spared so many times. Why?

During the course of my lifetime, I had quite a few brushes with death. I often wondered just what my purpose in life really is. What is my calling? Have I missed my chance to achieve something great? To put it another way: Have I not fulfilled my purpose in life?

I've been a "disaster waiting to happen" since I was a youngster; I'm talking elementary school. The second house we lived in backed up to the woods in our town of Irving, Texas. This was no small patch of trees. There were foxes, raccoons, and other various and assorted critters in there.

That place was one adventure after another until they began bulldozing the trees to make room for another subdivision. Take away the trees and bushes and what's left? Dirt. What can you do with dirt? Dig tunnels. I don't remember how deep we dug those tunnels, but I do remember we had several rooms in each tunnel. We had quite a network going on back there. We were quite young; the oldest one of us was probably in the third grade. I feel a need to stress our age because when you're that young you don't think about being buried alive due to the walls caving in, but one thing we should have thought of was the heavy machinery. You know, the bulldozers and graders, they were still there. This probably doesn't count as a brush with death because we weren't actually in the tunnel when the bulldozer ran over our new hangout, but we figured out real quick we had better find something else to occupy our time.

I stayed relatively calm for a while. The next six to seven years I was what you might call "subdued." Once I turned fourteen years old my adventurous side returned with a vengeance. I choose to describe what I did as *adventurous* because "stupid" seems a brutal way to describe a thrill-seeker such as myself.

When I was fourteen, a good friend and I used to sneak out of my house at night. When he spent the night we would say "good night" to my parents, go upstairs, and wait for them to go to bed. As soon as we deemed it safe we would climb the window onto the roof toward the front of the house and jump.

It worked great except when something went wrong. The night we decided to ride down the street on the hood of a car something went wrong. Actually I was fine. My friend, however, wasn't so lucky; he didn't stay on the hood. I thought for a minute all of that rolling was pure drama but it wasn't. He was really hurt. I personally didn't think he should have been in the hospital that long, but I wasn't a doctor so who am I to say. He did mention to me in passing that when they scrubbed the wounds to prevent infection there was some discomfort involved. The priest came to visit him and so did some of the girls from our class. I was beginning to think he was a bit of an opportunist. I was the one that had to explain to my parents just how it was my friend got injured without leaving the house. We returned to my house and went back to my room before I told my parents. That was no small feat. I always felt like I deserved more than I got. My friend didn't have to deal with the situation at my house, as his parents came and took him straight to the hospital.

It was a good year or two before I was involved in anything else remotely dangerous. To put it another way, I didn't have any close calls for a couple of years. You know how they say things happen in threes? There could be some truth to that. In my case it would have been fours or fives!

The next two years were chock-full of adventure. I suppose the first mishap would have been agreeing to race down a city street while parked at a stop light with a cop right behind me. (I never checked my rear-view mirror. I had no clue that a cop had the front row seat). The light turned green and we took off. I did have a fast truck. I smoked the tires and left the other guy and the cop sitting in a cloud of smoke.

Then I saw the lights on the police car.

As I reflect on this, I didn't want to race. I had a firm policy; I would not race with anyone else in the vehicle. My girlfriend wanted me to race; she was the instigator in all of this. Once I saw the lights I hit the brakes, the other driver saw this as an opportunity to beat me so he keeps bringing it on. Then, I'm guessing here, he must have also seen the lights because once he caught up to me he pulled over. I was in the lane he pulled into. He hit my truck, which sends my girlfriend and I over the curb. She comes flying out of the seat onto the floorboard while I'm mowing down mailboxes like I'm being paid for it. Her tater tots with ketchup were flying everywhere. We finally come to a stop less than a foot from a telephone pole and the cop (agitated beyond words) pulls me out of the truck and puts the cuffs on me.

My girlfriend was okay—when she was thrown to the floor it was probably the best thing that could have happened to her. It beats me how she got to the floor. By all rights she should have gone through the windshield or at the very least I would have expected her to hit the dashboard face first. That's why I wouldn't race with anyone else in the car. That scared me to death. Not my getting hurt, but her. She was my first love and my best friend.

The rest of the story isn't very exciting. The cop had another car come and take my girlfriend home, and he took the cuffs off of me and followed me home. He told my mother I was very polite and very cooperative. The other guy had his truck towed and almost ended up with a charge of assault with a motor vehicle. I begged the cop not to arrest him. It wasn't intentional and I was as guilty as the other guy. He ended up giving both of us a ticket and a stern (but good) lecture.

A couple months later I was out racing three-wheelers with some friends of mine. On the way back from our weekly "buck out" (I rode bulls in high school. A buck out was what we called practice) we decided to stop at a local track that rented three-wheelers by the minute. It was a pretty good sized track, fairly wide. Probably not wide enough for four three-wheelers going full speed around the curve at the same time, but it was a good sized track. I know it wasn't wide enough for all four of us. When you go around the curve at a decent rate of speed on a dirt track, the back tires are going to slide in whichever direction the three-wheeler is moving. The guy on the outside could possibly run out of real estate and that in fact is exactly what happened.

Once I hit the tires I was airborne. I went flying; the three-wheeler is rolling and comes to a dead stop with its roll bar in the middle of my chest, breaking my sternum. After I caught my breath I had a decision to make. Do I go to the emergency room where my mother is the head nurse, or do I go home and hope for the best? I did the respectable thing. I had my friends take me home. Being a good son, I wanted to save my mother the trauma of seeing her son wheeled into the emergency room. Chivalry was still alive and well in Irving, Texas.

Are you beginning to notice a pattern here? I'm not talking about my being a thrill-seeker. Do you think someone is looking out for me? Maybe my being hurt was supposed to be a learning experience. As you're about to find out, I'm a slow learner.

I would say it was another couple of months and I was riding in a school-sponsored rodeo in Haltom City, Texas, where most of our rodeos took place. This was my second and final year of riding as I was a senior. To give you some background I was not a good bull rider. I was too big. The best bull riders are short. They have a lower center of gravity. This, however, did not stop me from competing. Talk about an adrenalin rush! Bulls are just massive raw power—they are unbelievably strong. There were several times I got bucked off and wouldn't have a clue where I was. That happens to everyone, you hit the ground with such force it can leave you stunned at times. It just so happens on my last ride I was injured. I got stomped in the back; I liter-ally couldn't walk for two days. The bull didn't mean to stomp me. I had fallen underneath him and when he came down I was between him and the ground. That hurt; that hurt a lot. Again I didn't tell my parents the full story out of respect. I didn't want them to worry. Besides, they had a softball tournament to attend, which gave me two days to recuperate.

Not too terribly long after that I'm out cruising with a friend of mine. You know, we were riding around town, listening to music, drinking beer, and checking out the local hangouts. This night was no different than any other until we began fighting over something. I can't remember what it was but we both wanted it and it happened to be in the back seat. I'm turned sideways trying to grab whatever it was and he (the driver) was pretty much sideways himself.

The whole time we were wrestling over whatever it was, neither of us gave a second thought to the fact that he was supposed to be driving. We were so involved in securing whatever it was that we failed to notice when we ran over the curb. It would have probably been too late, but he may have been able to avoid the truck. We came to a screeching halt underneath it. At present there are laws that require trailer manufacturers to install a D.O.T. bumper about 20 inches or so from the ground to prevent cars from going underneath the trailer. But at that time, there was no bumper. The car went underneath the truck and stopped when the rear of the truck was a couple of inches from my shoulder. I couldn't turn around. I had to squirm a little to get back to the proper position. How many times can one person cheat death or at least serious injuries before it's not considered luck, and must be attributed to Divine intervention?

A year later—between high school and my first attempt at college—I was out water skiing with a friend of mine. He didn't have a ski boat; it was a small bass boat but we used it for both. I used to do all kinds of stunts on the skis. I was okay at skiing; actually he and I were both pretty good. I used to jump the wake, come out of the skis, and go skidding or sometimes rolling across the water. I'm not sure why but it was fun. My friend said it looked cool and I usually only ended up with a few bruises, so what the heck. I was doing that same thing one time, but when I came to a stop I stood up in water just over my knees. That could have easily killed me or at the very least left me paralyzed.

On another occasion, in the same boat on the same lake, I decide to yank the rope out of my friend's hand. We would do this to each other occasionally for a good laugh. What you do is turn toward the skier to create slack in the rope and then cut out of it and pull the slack out quickly. I was attempting to get even with him. Everything went according to plan until he put the rope in the middle of his arm, locked his elbow, and leaned back. Just after the slack came out of the rope the boat came out of the water and began to turn sideways. I thought the boat was going to flip over so I jumped in the water and by the grace of God I had removed my life jacket just before I started pulling him.

As I started to come up for air, I heard the motor getting closer. Then I saw a white patch coming toward me. I immediately changed direction and tried to go deeper. As you know, that's hard to do. As soon as I felt the current on my feet I curled into a ball. I felt the swirl from the prop as it passed over my feet. I swam deeper then headed for where I thought shore was. I told myself I wasn't coming up until I ran into the shore. That's what I did. I swam until I hit the bottom with my face at which point I stood up in water that was waist deep.

As soon as I broke the surface I could hear my friend yelling for me, there's another boat with two people yelling for me, and his boat is still going in circles. What a mess. That was a weird sensation. I'm almost on shore and people are looking for my body probably fifty yards out. It was far enough that no one could hear me. I had to keep waving my arms in the air until the people in the other boat saw me. I don't know how I survived that; I am not exaggerating at all. Adrenalin, I'm sure that's some of it. I know God has always been there for me. He's put up with my antics for a reason. There must be a purpose for my still being here.

Chapter Two

THE ENTERTAINMENT BUSINESS

Touring with Broadway Shows

The vast majority of entertainers I meet are godless people. I can't speak about *all* entertainers, but most of the crews I've met are godless as well. I think the local crews were better grounded, as most members had families at home who lived in the real world.

I didn't really spend any time with the local crews other than conversations in passing, but there's usually a little tension between the locals and the roadies. The road crew thinks they know everything and are usually very arrogant. The local crews quite often resent the roadies, and I don't blame them. As a matter of fact, I can't remember one theater at which we ever played where the local crew was any good. During every break, the roadies would tell me how awful the local crew was. My standard reply became, they're worse than the last crew which was worse than the one before that? The answer was always yes, they never got it. The roadies never considered for one minute it could have been their attitude. Maybe their expectations were too high. Just because the road crew had been handling the same set for the last year and a half doesn't make the local crew familiar with it.

I had a friend who drove one of the tour buses. He always said he should write a book about the entertainment business and title it "Between the Stage Door and the Dumpster" because according to him that's where all the action is. He was right. Sad to say it, but he was right. The things I've seen and heard are unbelievable. The only thing that can top that is one of their parties.

Think of the wildest party you've ever been to or heard of. I guarantee you it's nothing compared to the parties they have. It doesn't matter what you think you've experienced, you're minor league. Here's the difference—here's the reason I know I'm right. When you have no fear of God, when everything is acceptable, there are no boundaries because there are no such absolutes as right and wrong. Nothing is as it seems; reality is what you make it.

In the entertainment business you have to accept "gay" people. Perhaps that's the wrong terminology. In the entertainment business you're expected to cheer on the "gay" lifestyle. You're supposed to nurture them and tell them how unfortunate and oppressed they are. I was around it so much it seemed normal. I never condoned it, but it was everyday life. When I was away from it for awhile, I realized how far from normal they really are. I'm not referring to the gays in particular but everyone in the entertainment business. They live in a make-believe world so removed from reality I think, for them, reality itself became distorted.

A lot of them would emphasize to me that they didn't believe in God. Some would say they were reformed; they no longer practiced their faith. They had nothing to do with church. You know, "spiritual," but not religious. Actually, not even spiritual, I would say they were dead inside. I can easily recognize that condition because I've been there. As sad as it is to say, I met quite a few people who had never been inside a church. Can you imagine?

To get along in the entertainment business you generally must have the attitude that everything is okay. If everything is okay, something has to give. Unfortunately, most of the time it's your conscience, which quite often is linked to the Ten Commandments. Once you get rid of your conscience, when everything is acceptable, you are then qualified to decide what is acceptable to God. The ones who said they believe in God really think He's okay with their actions. Again, because everyone around you believes the same thing, it becomes normal and reality is distorted. There's a difference between tolerance and acceptance. Those on the left say they're open minded. I must disagree. Try opposing the view they expect everyone to live by. All of a sudden you're homophobic, judgmental, and racist, or anything else that comes to mind. Basically if you have a conscience and you exercise it from time to time, you're a problem. I personally never said anything to them about their behavior; instead, I quite often would stay away.

I am drawing on conversations I've listened to regarding their opinion about the "religious right" and so on. I had a lot of friends in the entertainment business, and on the surface they're as nice as can be. Really that's all there is: surface. They have no depth. Most of them are very shallow people and extremely self-centered. They are happy with government programs, because most of them could care less about the less fortunate. They would rather have the government take care of their fellow man leaving them free to do whatever. They did their part and voted for another government program.

I was walking down the street with one of the crew members in a large city where there happened to be a great number of homeless. One of the homeless approached us and asked for any spare change we might have. As I checked my pockets, the crew member abruptly said "no" and made his getaway as if the poor guy had some deadly contagious disease. As it turned out, I didn't have any change to give him. I should have given him folding money, but this was before my reconversion.

The point is that the other guy refused to even look; he refused to act concerned, yet he was one of the most politically correct people on the crew. The way he talked you would expect him to get some major humanitarian award, but the way he acted was just the opposite.

Shortly after my father was diagnosed with cancer, a woman in an entertainment-related business I knew said she would light a candle for him. After she said this I began to laugh. She said, "You're Catholic, you of all people should know what that means." I replied that I knew exactly what it means, which is why I'm laughing. How can you light a candle for my father when you yourself don't even attend Mass? Words mean nothing to them. As long as it sounds sincere, that's really all that matters.

God had a plan for me. I sometimes think He wanted me to experience the entertainment business in its entire splendor, behind the scenes and uncut. The entertainment business is where I bottomed out. It was during this time I made it to church more often than not. In fact, I would say it was my going to church that began to influence my way of thinking. All of a sudden, that line between right and wrong slowly began to reappear. Yes I was living in darkness, but as the line became more defined I realized where the darkness was coming from. Once we allow the line between right and wrong to get blurry, everything has to become darker so the line blends in. It's also true that once we begin to regain our moral bearing, the light reappears, which enables us to more clearly see the line.

It was while on tour and it became increasingly difficult to make it to church that I wanted out. Although when I was able to attend Mass I couldn't go to Communion, most of the time I had a need to be there. I still wasn't leading the life that would get me beatified but a change was beginning to take place. This really was a defining moment in my life; I could have gone either way. I made a lot of contacts in the entertainment business. I also drew closer to God. I deeply desired a relationship with Christ. Church was the only place I felt happy. It seemed the world stopped while I was in church—nothing else mattered. The entertainment business isn't real. The Father, Son, and the Holy Spirit—they're real. I chose God. I needed and wanted God in my life.

Where do I go from here? What can I do? I knew I had to stay in the trucking business as the truck market had crashed and my truck wouldn't bring what it was worth. As much as I wanted out of trucking, it may well have been part of the plan. When I'm on the road I have nothing but solitude. I became so very close to God by being on the road precisely because I don't have the normal distractions most people have. I can't plan anything unless I take time off, so most of the time it's just God and me. Jesus Christ has been most active in my life.

I used to read a chapter in the Bible, when I had time, from whichever page happened to open. Next I began reading one chapter every day in sequence, with the intention of reading the entire Bible. From there I progressed to reading a chapter a day in the Old and New Testaments. Then I discovered that the book of Psalms is the language God speaks. Another way to put it is that God prefers to communicate in the style in which the Psalms are written. Strangely enough, the book of Psalms was probably my least favorite of the entire Bible because it's much too close to poetry. However, after learning what God prefers, I took it upon myself to learn a "new language." Now I read a chapter in both the Old and New Testaments and also one psalm each day.

That's the Bible, but I also pray the Chaplet of the Divine Mercy each day at 3:00 and pray the rosary each night before I watch a lecture on either the history of the Catholic Church or the Gospels. I am in no way exalting myself but I am trying to illustrate just how important God has become in my life.

I don't really think for a minute it was God's plan for me to experience the entertainment business, as the entertainment business can in many ways be described as evil. God will never ask any of us to do anything that could in any way lure us away from Him. I do think His Son through the Blessed Mother and the Holy Spirit threw me a lifeline. Christ rescued me from myself and Satan; my path to reconversion was preplanned by Christ for my benefit. It was a slow process, but Christ finally got me safely on board. I'll say this: I have no intention of jumping, falling, or being pushed overboard. My life is with Christ. Wherever He needs me is where I'll be.

All I want out of life is to make Jesus Christ and His Father proud of me.

Chapter Three

STRANGE HAPPENINGS

I've never given much thought to the spirit world.

I always thought there was something to it. Beyond that, however, I really haven't given it much thought. I'm not referring to ghosts or anything like that. I suppose their existence is possible, but like everyone else I've heard my share of ghost stories and some are quite convincing. I once worked at a hotel in San Antonio, Texas, that is supposed to be haunted. I heard some weird noises on several occasions late at night but I never saw anything. There were stories of guests being thrown out of bed in a certain room, but here again I never saw anything and I never met any of the guests even though it was reported to have happened while I worked there.

When I refer to the spirit world, I'm referring to God and the angels vs. Satan and his demons. This I've always believed in but never really dwelt upon. Let's face it, that stuff happens to other people. Since I began writing this book I saw a couple demonic spirits. However, this book is about my relationship with Jesus Christ and ultimately God as the Blessed Trinity; therefore, if Satan is jealous, he'll have to find someone else to write about him as I could care less how he feels about it.

The first strange event happened one evening while I was driving down highway 39 through Illinois. I remember it was winter; not that it was extremely cold, but because it was still getting dark early. I had just eaten and was heading down the road feeling lonely—not for human company but for spiritual comfort. At this time in my life I was just getting reacquainted with God.

I had recently shifted from trying to read a random chapter in the Bible each day to committing to read one chapter every day until I finished the Bible. I started with the New Testament and then would finish with the Old Testament. I've always enjoyed reading the parables and healings of Christ, so I started with Him and ventured forth from there. One thing is certain from the moment you show a genuine heartfelt interest in God, things begin to happen.

As I said, this particular night I really felt alone. I don't remember what was going through my mind but I do remember being in deep thought, I know it had something to do with Christ or His Church. As I'm driving along, my radio came on and a voice came through the speakers. I recognized the voice but didn't know the person's name. Come to find out, the voice belonged to Father Corapi who I saw on TV before while visiting my mother. I remember having immediate respect for him (at the time before his unfortunate demise from the priesthood), not because he was a priest, which is reason enough, but because of how knowledgeable and confident he was in what he discussed. The station was EWTN, which to the best of my knowledge I had never listened to on the radio before. I'm not even sure I knew EWTN broadcasted over the radio.

I really wish I had written the different events as they happened. In my defense I didn't recognize then what would be the beginning of a wonderful—and to me a remarkable—journey of events that I pray never end. As the program ended, the radio went silent. The radio didn't turn off; it just went silent, no static, no nothing, just silence. Since that time on two different occasions, I've tried to tune in EWTN in that same area and could never get it. I've listened to EWTN in the Chicago area and I've heard Father Corapi. His show comes on around 10:00 or 11:00 in the morning, not the evening. How strange is that?

The second event was no less astounding but at the time I still didn't get it. You have to understand something: when these things happen it seems normal. I don't sit around and wait for them to happen, nor do I think about it. They just begin to happen. I was driving through southern Illinois and I felt stressed. There wasn't anything going on in my life that would cause this but for some reason my heart felt as though it would jump out of my chest. Maybe it was a panic attack; I don't know because I've never had one of those either. Whatever it was I didn't much care for it. I was beginning to get concerned because my heart was racing and I had not a clue why.

This time I was listening to the radio and all of a sudden a voice comes on, saying, *"Feeling stressed? Take a deep breath through your nose and exhale slowly through your mouth. Take a deep breath through your nose and exhale slowly through your mouth."* Then the music came back on. There was no, *this message brought to you by...* or anything like that. Obviously I did what the voice instructed me to do, and my heart slowed down. But really, what are the chances? As I began to think about these different occurrences I realized they can't be coincidental; as you'll learn elsewhere in this book, there were far too many.

I truly believe—scratch that—I *know* God chose me to help Him with His ongoing mission to save souls. Although I know God the Father has never spoken to me directly or in my dreams, I do know that God the Holy Spirit has, and Jesus Christ has even more so. There is a definite difference between the ways Each communicates, or to put it another way, you're left with a different feeling. When the Holy Spirit communicates with you it's like a teacher. Think of your favorite teacher, priest, relative, or someone in authority who you really respected and learned from. Then multiply that by infinity and this is pretty much the impression the Holy Spirit leaves with you.

Christ on the other hand, leaves an impression of love and mercy. He leaves with you a love that is so deep there are no words to describe it. If I ever came across someone who talked as Christ, I would immediately consider that person naïve, but with Christ this isn't the case. He is actually speaking with complete innocence and no sin whatsoever. That has to be the difference. Obviously there is no way He could ever be considered naïve, first and foremost because of who He is, and also because of what He's been through. He conveyed to me the disappointment He feels when we sin.

I can't explain how this communication with Christ made me feel, but I remember waking and feeling as though I was in a trance for most of the day. I remember looking at my mother whom I was visiting for Christmas and telling her that nothing on this earth matters. It was from this experience I learned that Christ's number one interest is the salvation of souls.

The Blessed Mother and the Holy Spirit will lead us to Christ, who will in turn introduce us to His Father. All Christ wants to do is share the joy and love of knowing His Father. Knowing how deep Christ truly loves us makes the comprehension of God the Father almost impossible for me. To me God is Jesus Christ and the Holy Spirit to a greater degree, if that makes any sense at all.

While I'm thinking about it, if anyone ever tells you that Christ or the Holy Spirit talked to them or put something on their heart, and that message has a secular ring to it, be suspicious. From my experience, limited as it is, secularism never enters into the conversation. In fact you're left with an overwhelming feeling that Christ could care less about anything secular. Secularism is a distraction; secularism will not help you get to heaven. In fact it may well keep you out. I'm confident when I tell you the Holy Trinity has tunnel vision. The most important thing to them is getting as many souls to heaven as possible; beyond that not much else matters.

I feel compelled to share another experience with you as this recently happened. The year of this writing, 2011, is a record year for snowfall in many parts of the country. There was a storm during the first week of February that was supposed to be 2,000 miles wide. I took a trip that originated in Bruce, Mississippi, and ended in Seattle, Washington. This meant I was going to travel diagonally through the storm.

I was really worried about this trip, so I prayed to God and asked Him to keep me safe. After I picked up the trailer, I decided to spend the night in West Memphis, Arkansas, as they were expecting an ice storm that night. The next morning, I walked into the truck stop and noticed the parking lot wasn't frozen. This was a good thing. I ate breakfast and headed out, but not forty miles down the road I began to come across jackknifed trucks. A couple of them had rolled over in the median, several cars were in the ditch, and it looked like a war zone. I continually thanked God for keeping me safe as I drove on dry road. This scene repeated itself throughout the day, but for all practical purposes I never hit a patch of ice.

As I got into Colorado, the highway signs warned about ice on the road. When I had to go inside at the port of entry, I inquired about the condition of the road. They said the roads were pretty icy as they had just had an ice storm themselves. The wind was blowing hard with gusts over 40 miles per hour. All I needed was to get caught on ice and get hit with a gust of wind. The load only weighed 3,000 pounds, but a 40 MPH wind could easily cause me to jackknife.

I offered the condition report up to Christ and took off. I never hit any ice; in fact, the road was dry the majority of the way through Colorado. Wyoming, however was a different story. It was my original intention to go up highway 25, then take 80 west, but there were road hazards and warnings in Rawlins. So, I elected to keep heading north and catch highway 90. You really have to watch the weather in Rawlins because of where the town is situated. The rest of the state can be sunny and Rawlins might be pushing blizzard conditions.

Anyway, I made it to Casper and quit for the day. I thanked God, said the rosary, and went to bed. I was watching the weather the next morning and knew I was going to be in for it. Idaho was good, but between Casper and Idaho were a lot of snow, hills, and Montana with a mountain pass on the Montana-Idaho border. The road was pretty icy but for most of the trip I managed to keep at least one side of the truck on pavement.

I was approaching the foothills and saw a huge, dark cloud at the top of the first hill. "Ominous" seems to be the appropriate word. I was watching the cloud for probably twenty miles or better, and I could see where the cloud began, but I couldn't see where it ended. The closer I got the bigger it got; I could see the snow coming down. This must be the worst part of the storm. As I began to climb the hill, the road disappeared into the cloud. I just knew I was going to get slammed with one heck of a snowstorm as I topped the hill. The truck, I'm sure, literally disappeared into the cloud because all of a sudden I'm in the cloud. The snow is coming down, causing white-out conditions about a quarter-mile to the west. Again I'm on dry road watching one heck of a snowstorm. I began to laugh and told God He was amazing and also thanked Him repeatedly. When I got on highway 90 headed west, I hit a few flurries but nothing like what I watched to what was now my south. At this point I'm literally circling the storm.

Just a couple days prior to taking this trip, I promised God I would quit stretching the truth (lying) in my logbook. Long-distance truck drivers are required to account for every hour, broken down in 24-hour periods, with restrictions for on-duty and driving hours. This is important to remember because what I'm about to share with you is no less miraculous. Every half-hour I would tune in the weather radio and continue to track the storm. According to the radio, the storm is almost non-existent west of Billings, Montana, which is good news. If I can get to the west side of the state near Missoula, or at least Butte, the temperature is considerably warmer. Of course this would mean adjusting my logbook, but it would be okay because in the end it works out better for me.

Well apparently, the good Lord didn't see it the way I did, especially since I promised Him I would no longer lie in my logbook. I was going to run out of hours in Bozeman, Montana, and about ten miles east of Bozeman the snow started coming down, the road disappeared, and the snow was getting deep. It was becoming very difficult to see, that was the longest ten miles I've driven in a long time. There was a truck stop in Bozeman and I headed for it. That night the temperature dropped to 20 below. I'm not sure if that was with the windchill or not because I was there another time when the mercury dropped to 30 below. Either way I've always maintained that once the temperature gets below zero, it's much too cold to be outside if you're not dressed for it.

The moral of this story should be considered. When I should have been up to my knees in snow, I'm on dry road. When I should have been out of the storm, I'm knee-deep in snow, all because I considered going back on my word. Christ must have viewed that as a teachable moment for me because I certainly learned a valuable lesson that day.

Christ Himself might say to us, "The end will never justify the means." He certainly said it to me. No matter how small or insignificant something may appear to be on the surface, the bottom line is, *what's wrong is wrong* and what's right is *right*—end of story. There are no footnotes or exceptions anywhere in the Ten Commandments either. In the end, there is right and wrong.

I'll give you another example of Christ constantly helping me to become a better person. Before I start, let me say this, it seems as if Christ works on one bad personality flaw at a time. I constantly pray and ask Christ to make me the person He wants me to be, and I truly believe He fully intends to do it with or without my cooperation. I have a habit of judging people based on looks alone. To me it's nothing serious and always in my mind; nevertheless, this apparently was a teachable moment.

One day, I was proved wrong, I bet five times at least. I don't necessarily always think something bad and quite often I get a laugh out of it, but nonetheless Christ doesn't care for it. Anyway it went like this: I would see someone and come to a conclusion about what I perceived to be that type of person. Literally, I would no sooner complete my thought and something would happen, instantaneously proving me wrong. Every time, the people were exactly the opposite of what I envisioned them to be. This went on all day; finally I smiled and said, okay, I get it. I shouldn't judge by appearances, and I'll quit doing it.

This has been a little harder to quit as it's a mental habit which, without realizing it, I've probably been doing most of my life. If I begin to make any assumptions about anyone, and if I don't catch myself and immediately apologize, He proves me wrong again. I'm getting better and I've almost broken myself of the habit, but I tell you He's persistent.

Christ truly is my best friend and I mean that with all sincerity. I was never more content or happier in my entire life. However, Christ has seen to it that I'm truly dependent on Him. When I realized what was going on, I literally told our Lord I never took a vow of poverty, but it's my opinion that my vow of poverty came by proxy. My bank account was literally drained almost overnight, or so it seemed. I'm not complaining; actually I sometimes laugh about it. I'll say this, I never worry about money or anything else, yet everything works out.

I'm not in any way suggesting that I enjoy a two-way dialogue with the Lord or that He communicates with me on a regular basis. What I would give for the chance to speak to Christ directly! Quite the opposite is true—I sometimes feel ignored. I do somehow sense His presence or that of the Holy Spirit; actually, I've physically felt the presence of one of Them on several occasions.

The first time this happened was while driving along highway 78 in Mississippi. It was a clear, calm night—nothing special going on—and I was listening to a CD of the New Testament. As I listened, I asked Christ to send the Holy Spirit upon me so I might understand more deeply what I was hearing. I no sooner finished speaking when my arms, legs, and back began to tingle and my seat began to rise (trucks are equipped with air seats which one can adjust, and the height can be regulated as well). Had I not been wearing the seat belt I may well have come out of the seat. I took this experience as One or the Other already with me. I've probably heard the New Testament on CD at least fifteen times and I neared the completion of my second reading of it as well. All I can say is, no matter how often I hear or read the Bible, I always come away with a deeper understanding. Through the grace of God my faith and knowledge continue to grow.

Now I will provide a very recent update. I drove from Clermont, Florida, to Tuscaloosa, Alabama, with no real good way to get there. I knew I had to take the back roads, which were okay with me. I decided to drive as far as McCalla, Alabama, which is just southwest of Birmingham and about thirty-five miles northeast of Tuscaloosa. This would enable me to miss the rush-hour traffic in Birmingham the following morning, while allowing me to sleep in at the same time. This was a real win/win situation for me.

The run itself was legal. I could drive to McCalla and be totally legal if I stopped once to eat and then kept after it. The problem is the client asked me to have the trailer washed and there were very few truck washes along the route I decided to go. I did stop to have the trailer washed at the last truck wash, at which time I was informed it would be about a two-hour wait. Not having much choice, I decided to wait and have the trailer washed. Once I was ready to leave again, I updated my logbook and realized I had to shut down around 7:15 PM, which meant I couldn't legally make McCalla.

I reasoned that since it would have been a legal run had I not stopped to have the trailer washed at the customer's request, I would adjust my logs in the morning and everything would be just fine. I wasn't concerned with fixing my logs immediately, as I would be in Alabama before my time expired. I knew Alabama didn't have any scales on the road I would be traveling.

Remember earlier, I stated *right is right* and *wrong is wrong*. All I can add to that is, *no matter what!* I was crossing the bridge from Georgia to Alabama right at 7:00 PM. I no sooner crossed the Alabama line when the trailer began to lose air pressure. I pulled onto the shoulder and noticed an air line was rubbing on the front axle and wore a hole completely through. Without sufficient air pressure the trailer brakes will not release. I tried to repair the line, but I didn't have any tubing.

Thus, my day was over.

I did manage to get the truck safely into a parking lot for the night. After calling and setting up road service for the morning, I realized what happened. I was in that parking lot at 7:15 PM, at which point my driving time expired for the day. Again, the good Lord held me to my word.

I apologized and told Christ I finally understood that our choices matter. Good or bad, we have to live with them and there are no do-over's. The act of a good deed does not entitle any of us to a free pass when it comes to sin. In fact, just the opposite is true: sin will erase the merit of a good deed. This doesn't mean we break even, or as they say, "no harm, no foul." Instead, this means we're in the hole, so to speak. We can never, under any circumstances, ever come out on top where sin is involved. Sin will never exonerate us from anything—it will always lead us to pain and suffering.

Chapter Four

CONFESSION

The lessons I learned

Throughout my journey, Christ has taken the opportunity to educate me at every turn. The lesson I received in Confession was nothing short of unbelievable. I had not been to Confession in probably thirty years because, as many other Catholics, I didn't find it necessary. I didn't really believe what the Church taught regarding Confession and grace. I mean really, if Protestants can repent on their own, why couldn't I?

There was a time in my life during which I quit attending Mass all together. I would say for a period of eight years, give or take, I hadn't set foot in a church. Whatever I learned about Confession was gone. Little did I know it wasn't only my memory regarding Confession that left me, I also lost whatever grace I had. I was virtually unprotected in a very cruel and evil world. I still believed in God but I was definitely living by my own rules. Who needs all those rules the Church put out? As it turned out, not only did I need all those rules, but as you will see, it isn't that the Catholic Church *made* these rules; rather, it's the Catholic Church which professes what the Holy Spirit proclaims.

I desperately needed God in my life. You would be hard pressed to find a picture of me smiling while I was on the outs. I never looked happy because I wasn't. I didn't know it then but I was empty. My soul was out of business, vacant, run down, condemned.

In a span of thirty years I had been married outside the Church twice. In between marriages there were quite a few girlfriends.

I never thought I had that many girlfriends but when I began to reflect on the subject it was sobering. I have two daughters from my first marriage who I raised without any help from their mother. The only thing I did right—my only saving grace—was that I sent them to a Catholic school for a couple years and we never missed Mass. My only accomplishment in life, the only accomplishment that matters, is that I did raise my daughters in the Church. Unfortunately there's more to being a Catholic than going to church. I could have and should have instilled them with a much stronger faith. I thought I was doing the right thing, but as it turns out you can't give what you don't have. The one rule I did remember—which, incidentally is the same one my mother wouldn't let me forget—is that I am personally responsible for my daughter's souls. This rule I did not then nor do I now take lightly. Until this day I'm still trying to correct my mistake, and my daughters are coming around. I thank God for that because my eternal salvation may well lie in the balance.

The closer I got to Christ the dirtier I felt. I knew I couldn't participate in the Eucharist until I went to Confession. Interestingly enough, before my relationship with Christ I would have told you I didn't need Confession because I wasn't doing anything that bad. For years I sat on the sidelines while most everyone else participated in the Body and Blood of Christ. I finally decided to make Confession a priority. In Wappingers Falls, New York, I had the opportunity to attend Confession.

I was nervous. What would the priest say to me? Would I be forgiven? Me personally, I didn't think I deserved forgiveness. Well, I went to Confession and confessed my sins. When I got to the part about being married outside the Catholic Church, he said one word to me: Why? This is hard for me to describe. When he asked me why, it wasn't that he wanted to actually know why I did what I did. The question was asked out of pain. He was disappointed in me; Christ was disappointed in me.

The priest gave me my penance, and then welcomed me back to the Church; after this he told me to recite the Act of Contrition. I knelt there like a dunce. I fearfully informed Father that I didn't remember how it went. I thought for sure my forgiveness just went out the confessional door. His reply floored me. He replied, I'll help you, I'll say it with you. I felt so much better. I had just lost 1,000 pounds. I was walking ten feet above the ground.

That euphoric feeling didn't last very long. I began to once again feel dirty. I wasn't sure why. I had recently been to Confession. I hadn't been a saint, but believe me, a Confession now would be downright boring for the priest. All of a sudden, events in my life began to creep back into my memory. Situations and people (women) I hadn't thought about in years were returning. Well, once again I quit participating in the Body and Blood of Christ. This time it really bothered me, and I could not go on like this. There was no way I could survive without the Body and Blood of Christ, no way, not again: I can't do it. The problem I had was I couldn't make it to Church every Sunday, much less Confession on Saturday, because of either work or the parking situation. If I had a trailer with me and couldn't find a Church within walking distance (two miles or less), I couldn't make Mass.

After feeling so unworthy for what seemed to be forever, I had the opportunity to attend Mass in downtown Rochester, New York. I couldn't make Confession but I could make Mass. The Cathedral was probably a mile and a half or so from where the trailers were parked, it was cold and windy, but that didn't really matter to me. As I was walking to Mass around the half-way point it began to sprinkle. I had a decision to make. Do I press on and hope the sprinkle doesn't turn into a downpour, or do I retreat and head back to my truck? Turning back briefly crossed my mind but I dismissed the thought. I was too close; no sir, I'm not turning back now.

The Cathedral was nice, but I wouldn't have cared if Mass was being held in a cardboard box. I was there! After the homily, which I remember feeling was specifically directed toward me, the priest said there were too many people not attending Communion, and your sins are forgiven. Right or wrong, the priest invited everyone to partake in the Body and Blood of our Lord Jesus Christ. Once again I'm ten off of the ground. What a night! Nothing could have upset me. I hadn't slept that good in months! The priest gave a general absolution but I realize now that he overstepped his boundaries, because he needed a grave reason to do so.

Again the euphoric feeling was gone. I lost the feeling really quick this time. What the heck is going on? I knew I hadn't sinned beyond my thoughts, if even that. I'm stumped. Am I a manic depressive? Should I consider therapy? This emotional roller coaster I'm on is getting old.

One day I watched a DVD of a priest giving a talk, and he said general absolution must be followed by individual Confession, especially as far as mortal sin is concerned. I knew immediately where my depression was coming from. Not soon after diagnosing my mental ailment, I made it to Confession in Harrisburg, Pennsylvania.

I had attended Mass in Harrisburg quite often. It was about a one and a half mile walk through downtown, but it wasn't bad unless the sidewalks were covered with ice and snow. I knelt in the confessional and mentioned to the priest that I had been forgiven for my sins through general absolution, yet continued to have a feeling of guilt. His reply was exactly the same as the priest in the DVD: You have to confess mortal sins through the sacrament of Penance in order to obtain absolution.

Well, he got an ear full. I was prepared this time. There's no way I'm going through this mess again; I'm finished with it. I've been close to Christ ever since. Am I perfect? No, I'm far from perfect. I do not commit—let me rephrase that—as of yet I haven't committed any mortal sins and with God's help I won't ever again. After this Confession I visited with the priest for awhile. I mentioned to him that I thought God was calling me to be a priest. He said that merely because I felt I was being called by God, it didn't mean I was being asked to become a priest. He did say he would pray for me that I might discern just exactly what it was I was being asked to do. At the time I was quite certain he was wrong, but as it turns out he was right. I was being asked to serve God, but in a totally different way.

My lessons were as follows: The priest truly is a vessel or conduit Christ uses during the sacrament of Penance. The priest is definitely in the confessional but he's what I consider a switchboard. During Confession, he gives you a direct line to Christ.

Make the most of it and come to appreciate the awesome gift of Penance.

The second lesson is no less important. Jesus Christ demands that we confess all mortal sins through the sacrament of Reconciliation in order to obtain forgiveness. The Catholic Church says you must confess all mortal sins through the sacrament of Reconciliation to obtain forgiveness. If this were a man-made rule, I wouldn't have experienced any feelings of guilt, especially since I wasn't aware the rule existed. I no longer simply believe in the power and grace of Reconciliation, I *know* the power of Reconciliation. I know the sacrament of Reconciliation is a gift from God through His Son, Jesus Christ, just as the Catholic Church teaches.

To reiterate an earlier point, when you make the choice to return to Christ He will see to it that you purge your soul. I've come to appreciate just how active Christ is in my life. As I've said many times throughout this book, Jesus Christ is literally my best friend. I can honestly say I live my life for Christ but by no means am I a fanatic. I don't for a second think that everything I experience is God's will but I know with all certainty every good thing comes from God. I can also truthfully say that most if not all of my prayers are answered and sometimes immediately.

The Lord and I have connected through the help of the Blessed Mother, Mary. I can't say I've actually had any contact with the Blessed Mother. It's my opinion that it was the Blessed Mother who asked her Son to take another look at me, as nothing out of the ordinary happened until I began to pray the rosary. I guess you could say I had a reconversion. If the Blessed Mother making an open-field tackle and knocking me flat on my back is a reconversion, then brother, I had one!

Prayer is the most effective and remarkable tool at our disposal. Consider making make use of it. If you are of the opinion that God doesn't hear you, it could be due to one of two reasons, which I will address soon. Allow me to establish one fact before I continue: God hears all prayers. Whether or not He acknowledges your prayer is up to Him.

The first reason your prayers may not be answered is because you're out of grace. I truly believe from my own experiences that you must find favor with God before asking for anything. God isn't a slot machine or better yet, a Genie in a bottle. He will not be used by anyone, and He has nothing to prove. You wouldn't ask a complete stranger for a favor, would you? First and foremost before you pray, check your soul and then approach God with the utmost humility. You can't fake humility; God will see right through you. If you haven't been to Confession in a while, get there as soon as you can.

The second reason you're not seeing any results could very well be what it is you pray for. If you pray for material goods for the sake of having them, you can hang it up. For example, let's say your car is dependable but it's just not stylish enough or it doesn't impress people. Too bad. What you don't need you won't get. This is my opinion, but the more materialistic one becomes, the further one drifts from God.

Another example would be if you're praying for a new job that will increase your income exponentially, but at the same time make it very difficult for you to attend Mass, you probably won't get any help from God. God will never help you move further from Him. You may indeed get the job and you may indeed have help, but I tell you this with total confidence: the help didn't come from God and you may well have placed your soul in danger.

Here are some examples of what has yielded some remarkable results for me. First, pray for yourself. With all sincerity and humility, ask God to make you the person He wants you to be. Be forewarned, God will take you up on this; in my case things began to happen almost immediately. Any prayer that has anything to do with the salvation of souls, especially your own, will always be answered. When you admit to God that you need His help, strap yourself in because you're most likely about to embark on the journey of a lifetime.

Ask God to take control of your life and then stop worrying and watch what happens. Will God test your faith? Probably. If you show faith in God He will come through for you and everything will continue to improve. Never forget that Jesus Christ had complete faith in His Father, yet He was still asked to die on the Cross. Unless you rank higher than Christ you may well be asked to shoulder a cross yourself, but continue to pray to God and you'll get through the worst of times. Don't always ask for favors in prayer, but sometimes ask the Lord how His day went, and be a friend to the Persons in the Trinity. Ask God what you can do for Him; again be ready, because you will get a response.

I highly recommend working for my best friend's Father doing whatever it is He asks you to do through His Son or the Holy Spirit. The pay isn't the best, but the rewards are out of this world. If Christ or the Holy Spirit ever communicates with you, your life will be forever changed. I personally spend the better part of my day in prayer or contemplating Christ and anxiously awaiting another interaction. I don't know if I'll ever have another Divine interaction but the possibility is enough to keep me going.

Christ said to those with the most, spiritually speaking, more will be given. This too has happened to me. My faith has grown by leaps and bounds, and the deeper my faith becomes the happier I am. I can say in all honesty that I awoke one morning much wiser than when I had gone to bed. It was shortly thereafter the amazing journey between me and Christ began. I've been given a job to do, it is my job to bring people back to the Catholic Faith, and it is my job to light a fire in the hearts of all who will listen. This isn't something I can put on a shelf and walk away from; no, this is now my mission in life. This is what is asked of me by my Best Friend, the one who saved my life.

Christ somehow creates a sense of urgency, I have to write and talk about God the Father, Jesus Christ, the Holy Spirit, and the Blessed Mother. People have to know who and what they're missing out on; people have to know that the secular life will get you nowhere quick. I can't stress enough the absence of a secular tone during any Divine communication; nothing on this earth takes precedence over the salvation of as little as one soul. If Christ is so concerned for our souls, it just can't be that easy to get straight to heaven.

Chapter Five

INTERACTIONS WITH CHRIST

1 This encounter wasn't exactly with Christ, but good did
win out over evil. I remember I had just gone to bed and
out of nowhere a feeling of imminent danger had come
over me. The only way to convey how I felt is for you to imagine
walking along in the dark, and in the blink of an eye you were
face-to-face with a wild animal, such as a wolf, lion, or a bear,
with no chance of escape. I have never in my entire life been that
scared or helpless. There was something in the truck with me. I
couldn't see it nor could I feel it, but it was there. I turned on the
lights and saw nothing. I looked out the window and once again
nothing. The fear hadn't left; in fact it became more intense. I
couldn't feel anything physical, yet I felt as though I was under
attack. This had gone on for hours. I desperately needed some
sleep as it was nearing midnight and I had to get up around three
in the morning.

I finally realized what was happening; it was Satan. He had
come to claim my soul for himself as for most of my life it
belonged to him. I prayed to Christ. I told Him that I had been
to Confession and was completely willing to serve Him however
He saw fit. I finally told Christ that I knew I was safe, and I knew
He would protect me. It wasn't even ten minutes and the feeling
of fear hadn't only left me, but I felt totally relaxed.

There was a fight for my soul that night, and God saved me.
He claimed me as His. I never knew that I was hell-bound. I
thought I was leading a fairly decent life. I know beyond the
shadow of a doubt that I was well on my way to hell. I know I've

been given a second chance at eternal life. I now have an intimate relationship with Christ. I feel His presence quite often and He lets me know in no uncertain terms that He hears me. The moment I let Christ know that I trusted Him completely and also surrendered myself to Him is when the feeling of impending doom left me.

2 There was another occasion shortly after the previous incident when Christ spoke to me. This also is hard to explain. There weren't any words spoken. I didn't hear anything with my ears. I wasn't asleep. What happened was all of a sudden, I knew that Christ through the Holy Spirit was asking me to help Him. I thought I was to become a priest. I remember jumping out of bed, I was actually excited. I told my family members, my daughters, and one of my friends. As time went by I couldn't figure out how I could pull it off. The Catholic Church, I would soon find out, prefers younger candidates for the priesthood. I was then fifty and figured it would take me close to two-and-a-half years to be in a position to go to the seminary. I began to wonder just what it was that Christ had in mind. I made some inquiries with different dioceses; I even emailed a priest from a religious order. I got no response from anyone.

I was angry for awhile, angry with the Church. Then I realized if Christ would have wanted me to be a priest, it would have happened. After all, He is the High Priest. I have no doubt He asked me to help Him, that was real. I just haven't discerned exactly what it is He wants me to do. I told Him on more than one occasion, if there is anything He wants me to do that He would have to hit me upside the head with a board because I won't pick up on a subtle hint.

3 The third time I knew Christ was speaking to me was in Kingman, Arizona, the night before I had prayed the rosary with so much emotion. Before I began the rosary, I was praying to Christ and asking Him to forgive me for not instilling my daughters with a stronger faith. I made no excuses for anything. Yes, I was a single parent. Yes, I would sometimes

work late hours. Yes, I was always tired when I got home. None of those matter; God is still number one. He should always be number one. When God is number one everything else falls into place.

Anyway, I had prayed so hard with so much intensity that there were tears running down my face, (this is amazing as I've been told on more than one occasion that I'm a cold so-and-so). After I finished praying the rosary I told Christ I loved Him and went to bed. I felt 100 pounds lighter, like a massive boulder had just been taken off of my shoulders.

The next morning I went inside the truck stop for breakfast, while walking I asked Christ if He was even listening to what I had been telling Him. As usual, I walked past the drivers section as I just wanted to eat and go, and I didn't feel like getting into any world-altering conversations. I felt refreshed but a little melancholy from the night before. Again I began wondering if Christ was listening to me. Where did I stand with my new Best Friend?

As it turned out I had to eat in the drivers section as the back of the restaurant was full. I had breakfast and got up to leave when the waitress brought the check over. She handed me the check but then snatched it from my hand. She wrote something on the back of it. I knew what it said; I'd seen it a hundred times. *Thank you,* picture of a smiley face, and then her name.

Well I turned it over and read it. It stated, "Jesus Loves You."

I couldn't speak. I wanted to tell her how that affected me but I was speechless. Coincidence, you might say? I would have thought that before, but not after everything else I had recently been through.

4 Another encounter with Christ is really interesting. I had just dropped a trailer in La Porte, Texas, and drove to a truck stop in Houston (twenty miles) so I could express-ship my paperwork out. There wasn't much on the load board; I was prepared to stay the night. I figured how much more I needed for the month to cover all of my bills plus some work I needed on the truck over Christmas. I thus figured I needed another $701.00, and I remember saying to Christ (I talk to

Him throughout the day) how nice it would be to be able to cover this before Christmas so I could enjoy the week at my mother's house without worrying about work. The year 2010 was not a good year for me, business-wise, and I didn't want to end the year with a losing month.

I was thinking about writing a book about my life from a religious perspective. You know, my life before Christ befriended me compared to now. I know Christ loves everyone. I know you have up until your last breath to accept Christ and repent. I know all of that. I know He's Jesus Christ the Son of God, the Messiah. I get the picture. What I didn't know, what I discovered is, He truly is my Best Friend.

Okay, back to the story. The problem with me writing a book is I don't know how. I remember in college I always had to read my stories to the literature class. After a while the professor took it upon herself to read them aloud after they were graded. Everyone seemed to like my stories and my writing style. You see, I've tried to write since then, but nothing happened.

This time, however, I picked up my tablet with the intention of writing an outline—you know, gathering my thoughts so I would have some general idea about that which I was contemplating. In about an hour I had identified sixteen chapters; those chapters were broken down even further with four to six different but related topics in each chapter! Everything was flowing. I didn't put forth much strenuous effort; instead, the ideas just kept coming. As I finished the outline I had a call. It was my broker, and she had a load to offer me. It wasn't the greatest but it got me out of town and I could turn it quick, so I took it. I got there and they had made an error, as they didn't need me. I drove twenty-three miles and was reimbursed $200 for the cancellation. Fortunately, there was a truck stop about ten miles down the road so it really wasn't a major ordeal. The upside was I now only needed $501 to cover everything.

Once I got to the truck stop I decided to check my email, and my other broker had sent me a load confirmation that had to be picked up in Beaumont, Texas, which was about sixty miles away. I put everything away and headed out. It was already 3:00 in the afternoon, and the place closed at five so I had to get with the program. Now normally I would have called and confirmed everything but this time I just took off like I knew what I was doing.

I looked at the clock and realized I needed to pray the Chaplet of the Divine Mercy. I got the book out of the glove compartment (I didn't have all of the prayers memorized as I had just started this practice the week before), grabbed my rosary, and gave it my best shot. The only thing more dangerous than drinking and driving is reading the Divine Mercy prayers, holding the rosary, and trying to shift at the same time. You'd think there would be a law against that! If that wasn't enough the phone rang. You guessed it, the load cancelled.

As soon as he told me, I literally put my blinker on and exited into a truck stop. It wasn't much more than a convenience store with a big parking lot, I had never been to this place but I needed somewhere to park so I could finish my prayers before 4:00. I parked the truck, went back to the sleeper, knelt down, and began to pray. The phone rings again. This time it's my youngest daughter. We talk for a little while and then I inform her that I have to go as I'm looking at the clock and time is slipping away.

Once again I'm kneeling down and I no sooner pick up the rosary than someone knocks on the door. I really don't want to answer the door as the clock refuses to stop and time continues to slip from my grasp. Because I don't want to be rude I go back up front, and there stands some guy with long hair, unshaven, and fairly well built. He looks me right in the eye and says, "Don't be afraid, I'm not dangerous." The strange thing about this is I stand six-foot three and weigh 245. I assure you, I wasn't scared. I put the window down and I'm all of a sudden overtaken by total calmness. This man was unshaven, his hair wasn't messy (but it wasn't combed), and he still didn't strike me as having bad hygiene. I felt as though I had known this guy all my life.

He repeated, "Don't be afraid, I'm not dangerous." I realized why he's saying this, as I haven't said anything. Again I'm speechless. I'm not sure who this guy is but he's not who he's presenting himself to be. He continued to speak.

"I'm trying to get to the west side of Houston. Another driver just dropped me off. I'm trying to gather some spare change.

It's a small truck stop. I'm just trying to put together enough money so I can get something to eat. I think I'm going to stay here tonight. You don't have to worry as I don't do drugs; I might have a drink now and then but I don't do drugs." I reached into my pocket and pulled out thirty-two dollars in bills, of which I gave him ten dollars.,

"Are you serious?" he exclaimed.

"Yes," I answered, "go get yourself a warm meal."

"A warm meal! I can get something to eat and something to drink, and still have money left over to eat in the morning. Thank you!"

At this point he extended his arm to shake my hand, as we shook hands he gazed into my eyes and said, "God bless you." He turned away, looked at the hood of my truck, placed his hand on it for a brief second and walked off.

When he said *God bless you,* he said it with conviction. He didn't say "may God bless you," he said God bless you like he knew God would indeed bless me. Well, he left and I had ten minutes to finish my prayers, so again I knelt down. This time I was successful in completing the task at hand.

After I finished praying I decided to go inside to see if this place had any laundry facilities. As I'm walking across the parking lot, I see the same guy walking out. I'm still quite some distance away and he wasn't looking in my direction so he didn't notice me. He had walked out the door, turned to his right, and then turned right again as if he was going to walk in front of the building. I went inside.

The front wall is solid glass but I couldn't see him. I walked through the facility without finding a laundry room. I decided to find this guy and invite him to dinner; I just had to know who he was. I went outside but couldn't find him. Somewhat confused about what had taken place, I went back to my truck.

I no sooner got in my truck than the phone rang. A different broker had called my own broker, and then called me to offer a load that I could turn in two days and clear a thousand dollars. At 5:00 in the evening you don't usually get a call from the east coast with a high paying load, especially when it's late. Believe me, that's not normal. God did indeed bless me.

I keep asking myself, did I meet Christ? Did I meet an angel? Who was that? I have never in my life felt that calm around another human being. There was definitely Divine intervention that day at the very least. Was God testing me? Obviously I prefer to think I met Christ. I'll never forget that day or his eyes. There was an aura about him; nothing but goodness emulated from him.

The way he spoke reminded me of the parables. To me, when I read the parables the one thing that always comes out is Christ's innocence. That's what this guy sounded like, so innocent, and so pleased in my giving him ten dollars. It wasn't the fact he received money that made him happy, he was genuinely rejoicing for me because I gave him the money. I'm constantly approached by people less fortunate than myself asking me for money. I would estimate the number of times I'm asked for money by a complete stranger each week is at least ten, but this experience was completely different.

There was something else about the way he was dressed. Not so much the way he was dressed but what he had with him. There was a white strap going over his right shoulder that was attached to something on his left hip. I'm not sure what it was. It was a cross between a purse and a satchel maybe, I don't know. At the top where the strap attached at each end it almost looked like a tube yet there was no separation from the top to the bottom. There clearly appeared to be a place to store something. It literally looked like it was designed to carry a scroll at the top. Lapping over the top was a flap which opened up the rest of the bag. The lower part resembled a saddle bag more than anything else. I've never seen anything like it; I have not a clue what it was. I know our paths will cross again and the next time we meet I will ask him where he's from. If he is who I think he is he won't be able to lie: Angel or Christ, it doesn't matter. On that day I'll know to whom I am speaking. I say I'll be prepared and that I'll know exactly what to say, but I'll most likely be left speechless again.

Chapter Six

VOTE PRO-LIFE

What I have been told by Christ

The first message I received from Christ was that the only way to end the hard times and all the turmoil is to vote pro-life. You see, because we as a nation have not lived up to our Judeo-Christian heritage, we are paying the price.

How can we expect God to show us favor as a nation when we have done everything to push Him away? Legalized abortion, in-vitro fertilization, no prayer in school, and the onslaught continues daily. All of this can be fixed with one simple action: Vote pro-life.

My Best Friend, Jesus Christ, went through unimaginable pain and suffering, and then died a horrific death to forgive us our sins. He did this so we might have eternal life in heaven with God, the Father Almighty. Quite often, especially when I'm praying the Sorrowful Mysteries, I thank Christ for what He did and then I tell Him that we're not worth it. We as Christians will vote for a "pro-choice" (anti-life) candidate if he or she sides with us on social issues. How many lives is each issue worth? Who gave man the right to decide matters of life and death?

How can you consider yourself to be Catholic, Christian, or Jewish and vote for any pro-abortion candidate? The Catholic Church called this one from the beginning. The Church not only was against the abortion issue but was also afraid of where it would lead.

Where did it lead? In-vitro fertilization, euthanasia, and worse! President Obama said in no uncertain terms that the

United States government is partnering with God in deciding who will live and who will die. As far as I knew, the only partnership having authority over life and death is the Partnership between God the Father Almighty, Jesus Christ the Son of God, and the Holy Spirit. It's time to be scared; it's time to be concerned. This country is so far off track that we have separation of Church and State in everything except death. When it comes to death, our government partners with God? By the way, separation of Church and State was intended to prevent the government from getting involved in matters of religion; it was never intended to force God out of the country. Read the Constitution. God was very much a part of the founding of this country.

If you vote pro-abortion, you're committing a mortal sin. Should you care to check the Commandments, buried about halfway down is number five and it states, Thou shall not kill. There are no footnotes; it simply states thou shall not kill. On the day of your judgment do you honestly believe that you'll be able to look Christ in the eye and say, I voted for the pro-"choice" candidate because it benefited me in other ways? Do you really think His reply will be, "Well, since you personally profited from the death of the hundreds of thousands of unborn children of which you were a party to, come on in, enter My Father's House." Of course He won't.

What social or monetary issue could possibly be worth your soul?

Christ willingly gave His life so that we might gain eternal life with His Father, God Almighty. Why then can't we protect the lives of the unborn? More importantly, why is abortion an issue? Have we as a society moved so far away from God that life and death have become social issues? Jesus Christ, the only Son of God, is asking us to vote pro-life and leave the rest to His Father. Is this too much to ask? Don't we owe Him our life? At first I thought this was my idea because as I was having a conversation with a friend of mine, I told him if we would all vote pro-life our problems would take care of themselves. After the conversation was over I began to wonder where that came from. This was nothing to which I had given any thought. Then the next message was, and I quote, "Stand with My Father and leave everything else to Him." Granted, the two messages were a couple of weeks apart, but I began to realize something spectacular was happening.

As I've mentioned elsewhere, the lack of a secular tone when Christ or the Holy Spirit communicates with me is something that can't be put into words. When Christ says to vote pro-life and His Father will take care of the rest, I don't know if He refers to finances or not, but my sense is the latter. I do know Christ is referring to moral issues and the steady decline of said morals in the United States of America as well as the entire world.

I'm quite sure any nation that makes abortion illegal will find favor with God. One can analyze and explain in great detail when and where the United States began to decline. I'm quite sure many can explain away our current dilemma without the mere mention of God and I'm just as confident the reverse is true for our road to recovery. However, I submit to you that we as a country take a step back every time we defy God. I further submit to you that this nation will not see true peace and prosperity until we as a nation return to our Judeo-Christian roots.

The only statement President Obama has ever made that I agree with a hundred percent is that the United States is no longer a Christian nation. He is exactly right! So many people were angered when he made that statement. I don't understand why. The first time he actually tells the truth he offends more people than when he fabricates a story. Where was the anger when the president said the government was partnering with God in matters of life and death? The truth hurts! Forwarding an email that has a religious tone does not make one a Christian. Being open-minded and voting for any pro-abortion candidate does not make one a Christian. Going to Mass or Sunday services does not make one a Christian. Satan not only believes in God but knows Him personally, yet he certainly isn't a Christian. Being spineless does not make one a Christian! Just because something is legal doesn't make it moral. Believe me, I was a model citizen on the expressway to hell. I didn't break any laws, yet I routinely broke the Commandments.

Here's the bottom line. If you think for one minute that you're not going to be judged by who you voted for, think again.

If you knowingly vote for a pro-abortion candidate, the blood of the unborn is on your hands as well, and you will have to account for your actions. Whether you agree with me or not has no bearing on what I just said; in fact, should you continue to vote pro-abortion, your problem has just been compounded because you can no longer claim ignorance as an excuse. If you strive to be popular and be accommodating to everyone in this life, you make all the more difficult the possibility of attaining eternal life. As Christians we're called to be tolerant and pray for those who are misled, but don't confuse tolerance with acceptance.

On a final note, if the sanctity of life doesn't persuade you to seek an end to abortion, euthanasia, or any other life-ending or altering practice, consider this; there is a difference between the life of a human and that of any other living creature. If you happen to be of the thought that abortion is okay so long as it's carried out within a certain time frame, consider this. God said He knew you before He formed you in the womb. How can this be? Even though God is God and we can't possibly comprehend how He thinks, it is only reasonable to assume that God must be referring to our soul. If this is the case abortion is not only murder but it's horrific at the very least.

The following I can state with complete confidence, having experienced this first hand. The Triune God is most interested in the salvation of souls. Christ has led me to understand that when an abortion is carried out, the taking of an innocent human life is one edge of the sword. The act of preventing a soul from embarking on the journey of life is just as horrific. This journey will hopefully culminate in the discovery of God through His Son, Jesus Christ, enabled by the inherent characteristics unique to the human soul, which is entrusted to each one of us by God Himself with the hope of it returning to Him through its own free will. The soul robbed of its normal journey on earth: Horrific! This is the greater of the two sins wrapped up in the practice of abortion.

It isn't possible to have an interaction with Christ and not be humbled and forever changed by His deep love and mercy for every single soul, as well as His intense passion for the salvation of all souls. In fact when Christ speaks (at least in my experiences), He never refers to people as anything other than souls. This alone should emphasize just how precious each and every soul is. Should you doubt what I just stated, do your own research and begin reading about the saints. You will soon discover three words that are common to most all of them: salvation of souls.

For this reason alone I fear for all souls on the wrong side of the abortion issue. I pray that they come to appreciate the sanctity of life and then seek refuge and forgiveness, love and mercy in the arms of Christ Himself.

Chapter Seven

ONE CHURCH

What I have been told by Christ

I t is the intention of Christ that there should be one Church:
The Holy Catholic Church. Christ did not die on the Cross
so man could come up with an additional 33,000-plus varia-
tions of Christianity.

We were given by Christ one Church: The Holy Catholic
Church. The Church was born from the side of Christ when He
died on the Cross. Before this, He did instruct Peter to feed His
sheep, and Peter with the help of the other Apostles, Paul, and
many disciples, began the apostolic ministry in what was then
the infant Catholic Church.

What cannot be duplicated by any man-made "religion" is
the interpretation of Scripture in addition to the sacraments.
Anyone can come up with a different interpretation, and many
have, but that doesn't make them right. Man being man, we
always think there's a better way. We always have a need to
improve or devise a shortcut. Our intentions may be good but
we don't always achieve the desired outcome.

The Catholic Church had its fair share of problems to be
sure, but the problems have been man-made and never purely
doctrinal. The Protestant split occurred because of the actions
of many of the clergy around the sixteenth century, but also
because there were some that didn't agree with the doctrine and
what now is commonly referred to as man-made rules. Again,
that might sound good but it doesn't make them right.

While most everyone had many legitimate reasons to be upset with the Catholic Church, there is no excuse for the changing of doctrine. As I read through the Catechism of the Catholic Church I found quite a bit of what I was told by Christ, including one Holy Catholic Church. In the Catechism it states that everyone is called to be in full communion with the Catholic Church. Prior to my experience I would have attributed that statement to pride or arrogance but I now attribute that statement to the Holy Spirit, as I do everything else about the Catechism and the Catholic Church. Christ has gone to great lengths to show me that which the Catholic Church professes is truly dictated and inspired by the Holy Spirit.

Whenever the pope, a curial Congregation, or a bishop from the Vatican states something, they seem to offend someone or some group. According to the Catechism, any person of any faith can make it to heaven. There are some Protestants who took issue with that statement. As is usually the case, they have heard what they want to hear. What the Church says is this: the closer you get to what the Catholic Church teaches the better chance you have of making it to heaven. By the same token, the further you stray from the Catholic doctrine the less likely it is you'll make it to heaven.

Christ has given His Church the Holy Spirit, Baptism, Penance, Holy Communion, Confirmation, Marriage, Holy Orders, Anointing of the Sick, His Mother, and all of the saints. The other Christian faiths have no sacraments. The road to heaven is much more difficult when you have less to work with. Christ gave, as a gift to the Catholic Church, each and every sacrament to aid us in our attempt to obtain eternal life with God, the Father Almighty.

It is through these sacraments and the grace bestowed upon those receiving each particular sacrament that God offers us the best chance to get to heaven. My best friend, Jesus Christ, is an authority on this subject. If He says it I believe Him. His desire is for each and every one of us to make it to heaven. Life is short; eternity is forever. We only have one life to get it right. There are no do-over's. If there's one thing that has been conveyed to me over and over it is this: it's not that easy to get into heaven. If the road to heaven were easy, Christ wouldn't have a need to convey His concern, would He?

The conversion to Catholicism will be over time and it will be gradual. It would seem that the first step will be the reunion of the Roman Catholic and Eastern Orthodox Church. The Church must be whole above all else and this will happen through the guidance of the Holy Spirit. Once the Catholic Church becomes one again, the Protestant faiths will begin to come back with the guidance of the Holy Spirit.

While it is Christ's intention that all Christians be of one faith, don't think for a second He won't be with us every step of the way. When this happens it will seem natural, this I know for certain. There's something about Christ. I'm not sure what it is but He makes the impossible and inconceivable seem like an everyday occurrence. In my opinion it is for this reason that Peter said on more than one occasion, "It is because of this we believe that You are the Messiah."

It seems to me that having the opportunity to be in the presence of Christ everyday would have lessened the impact of who He actually was. What I'm trying to say is whenever Christ would perform a miracle He would be so casual it would seem normal. Christ never did anything for applause but always out of love. Christ never forgot His purpose for being here and never lost focus. His purpose for being here was to draw people to His Father and the salvation of souls through His death and resurrection.

From experience I can tell you that as Christ is working in your life, whatever He does will seem normal, and you won't even give it a second thought. However, once you've arrived where He wants you, you'll look up and say *WOW*. You'll know it then and you'll be able to name every single work Christ accomplished for you. He did these works to get you where He wants you to be so He can use you to save souls. The bottom line will always come down to the salvation of souls: yours and those of others.

Chapter Eight

THE HAMMER AND THE NAIL
What I have been told by Christ

I find this so simple yet profound and enlightening. This, to me, explains it all. After you read this I'm sure you'll understand how this ties into Christ's message regarding the one Holy Catholic Church.

We're all born with a tool belt and a small hammer. This is our gift from God. As we get older we're afforded the opportunity to add additional tools to our tool belt. The first tool we put on our belt, hopefully soon after birth, is Baptism. The next tool available to us after Baptism is Penance. Between Baptism and Penance our hammers begin to grow and get a little heavier. The same is true for Holy Communion and Confirmation. By the time we've received Confirmation our hammer has more than doubled in size and weight.

As the years go by our hammer is getting larger and heavier. Our other tools should be getting larger and heavier also. If the other tools remain the same size as when you received them, or worse yet, begin to shrink, it will become difficult for you to walk. If the hammer is considerably heavier than the other tools you begin to have problems. If the hammer is on your right side you will be pulled to the right. If the hammer is moved to the rear of the belt it will make it hard for you to walk straight ahead and eventually you will have to stop. The same is true if the hammer is moved to the left side, you will be pulled to the left. Obviously as big as the hammer has become, there is no way you can put it on the front of the belt. If you did this you would surely trip and fall. No matter what you do, you will not be able to stay on the correct path, for the correct path is narrow and straight and you are unable to walk straight.

You must make sure that all of your tools grow together. If all your tools grow together, walking down the straight path will be much easier.

Sin is the nail. Whether or not we realize it, sin always causes us pain. I originally thought Christ was saying that our sin caused Him physical pain. This really bothered me because if that were the case, I personally caused Christ quite a bit of pain. I also began to wonder why the Catholic Church didn't mention this.

Before I submitted this book to the Bishop I asked Christ if I had written everything the way it was told to me. I also mentioned to Him that I was somewhat concerned about submitting something that the Church didn't teach, which prompted me to mention that I couldn't publish anything that wasn't approved by the Church.

Please understand I was in no way confronting Christ, but He has personally given me a tour of His Church from every angle and has shown me that everything the Catholic Church teaches is completely true. The doctrine is infallible and the pope can speak infallibly. Well as it turned out, I was wrong. I assumed because sin is the nail and our free will is a hammer, Christ must be saying in effect that it's like driving a nail into His hand, which He did indeed say, but Christ never said we cause Him physical pain. Christ was referring to His Passion: He died once for all.

A couple days after my praying to Christ, His reply was, and I quote, "the pain felt is not Mine." The pain caused by sin belongs to us as it should. We may not acknowledge any wrongdoing immediately, but eventually we will suffer for our sins either in this life or the next. The pain Christ feels now is that of disappointment and heartache, but nothing physical.

What does this mean? The tool belt is our conscience and the hammer is our free will, which are our first gifts from God. The size of the hammer is relative to our innocence and our faith in God. Obviously a newborn is innocent of everything except the stain of Original Sin, so the hammer is very small at first. As we get older we begin to exercise our free will more and more. The more we allow ourselves to drift from the teachings of Christ and His Church, the bigger and heavier the hammer becomes. Eventually we lose our ability to stay on the right path.

Picture this, if you will. A normal tool belt usually holds a claw hammer. The claw hammer isn't too big yet; it's heavy enough and big enough to create and build. Because the hammer is equipped with a claw in the event we make a mistake we can use the claw to remove the nail. Just as in real life if we stay within the teachings of the Church, when we sin we're able to exercise our own free will, attend Reconciliation, and as with the nail, the sin is removed through absolution.

On the other side of the spectrum, if our free will is allowed to develop unchecked, our claw hammer becomes a sledge hammer. Sledge hammers are almost always used for destruction. Sledge hammers are used for tearing down brick walls and destructively removing anything. In fact, you can't really carry a sledge hammer on your tool belt; it's much too big. You pretty much have to carry the sledge hammer over one shoulder or the other and it can become quite cumbersome after a while. Come to think of it, if your day consists of swinging a sledge hammer, you really don't need the tool belt. All it will do is get in your way.

Much is the same with our conscience. When we use our free will for evil, our conscience has to go, as it too will get in the way. There's not much point in keeping our conscience around anyway, as we're not exercising our faith by attending Mass, partaking in the Eucharist or in Reconciliation, so who needs it?

As Catholics we are held to a higher standard because we have all the tools necessary for eternal salvation.

I now understand just how much Christ loves each and every one of us. I can't put it into words because there are none that can describe His capacity for love and mercy. I guess the closest word I can use would be *infinite*. His love knows no bounds. It is unbelievable. Whenever Christ communicates with me, His deep love and mercy are somehow conveyed. This alone has humbled me to the point I sometimes don't recognize myself.

The thought of sinning really has an adverse effect on me these days. I'm not for a minute suggesting that I don't sin; in fact, it's quite the opposite. I'm keenly aware of my shortcomings, whereas before I really thought I was leading a good Christian life. But my sins are no longer premeditated. I pray and strive daily to not only avoid sin but most especially mortal sin. Venial sin is much more difficult to control because quite often it may be a passing thought or even a quick response to a given situation. However, mortal sin can be eliminated with much less effort.

I repeatedly mention to Christ during prayer that His will is my will. Whatever He desires of me or wherever He needs me all He has to do is ask. During prayer I'm constantly asking Christ for the opportunity to serve Him. I let Him know that all I want is a chance to make Him and His Father proud of me.

I sometimes wonder if all of this is real. But when I think about everything that has happened to me recently I have no doubt that it is real. I feel so fortunate to have such an intimate relationship with Christ. He truly is my best friend. Christ has given me a spiritual tour of His Church, enabling me to tell everyone without a doubt that I know the Catholic Church is His Church.

I know the Eucharist under the appearance of bread and wine is the Body and Blood of Christ. At some point we all have to move beyond belief, we have to *know*. If we all knew without a doubt that the Eucharist is the Body and Blood of Christ we wouldn't be so casual about receiving Communion and we sure wouldn't attempt to receive Communion while in need of Confession. I can tell you I wouldn't have gone for so long without receiving Communion. Better yet, I wouldn't have done most everything I did, had I truly known the Eucharist is indeed the Body and Blood of Christ.

If everyone not only believed but knew beyond the shadow of a doubt that what the Catholic Church professes is the truth, this world would be totally different. If only the Catholics believed that which the Catholic Church teaches to be the truth with no disclaimers or exceptions, the world would be a better place. As I've said before, if Christ is so concerned about everyone coming back to the Catholic Church, the journey to heaven must be much more difficult than most people would like to believe. Christ knows it is through the sacraments; through His Body and Blood we have our best chance at eternal salvation.

My advice: Aspire to be a saint, pray often, even several times a day. Love God above all else. If you truly love God, everything else will fall into place. When you love God with your whole being (mind, heart, and soul) you won't be capable of hating anyone. You will also find that you are much more forgiving. Attend Mass as often as possible, receive the Eucharist, and make Reconciliation a way of life. Make time for adoration and attend Benediction whenever you can. The bottom line is, put God first and you will see a dramatic improvement in your life.

I used to have a hard time putting God first. I didn't understand how I could love someone I didn't really know, more than I loved my own daughters. It was because of that attitude that the only people I loved, the only people I was capable of loving were those closest to me: mainly my daughters, my parents, and Aunt Billie. I'm convinced that if you truly love God with your whole being you also have to love everyone else. Is it because we love God that we love everyone else? No, I don't think so. It is because God loves us back that we love everyone else. It is God's love that radiates through us, which in turn makes us capable of loving our neighbor as ourself. The more your love for God grows, the more your faith grows, and the greater your capacity of love for your fellow man becomes. When you put God first you will naturally aspire to be a saint.

Chapter Nine

Catholicism

For far too long I took my religion for granted. Like many other Catholics, I would show up for Mass on Sunday and that was about the extent of my faith. What I just described is, in my opinion, the "average" Catholic practice. How disappointing, how utterly revolting.

We as Catholics are called to a higher standard. My Best Friend did not die on the Cross for our convenience. He did not give us the sacrament of Penance in the event, however unlikely it is, that we might fall into sin. Let me rephrase that, some have the opinion that in the event we're "forced" into a sinful situation, Jesus Christ gave us the sacrament of Penance. Sounds a little arrogant, don't it?

Most of us feel we no longer need Confession, which I assure you isn't due to perfection or humility; it must be arrogance, or worse yet, ignorance. Is the human leadership of the Church to blame for this? Yes, to a certain degree I believe Church authorities must shoulder some of the blame. However, you and I must take responsibility for our own salvation. Did the clergy get lax? Yes, quite a few of them did as most of us. The Catholic Church is one: When one of us is hurting the rest should come to his or her aid. When was the last time you prayed for the Church or the clergy? Me personally, until recently, I have never even thought about praying for the clergy.

The Church that Christ started has so much to offer that we as Catholics have no excuse. Do you know of any Catholic parish that has done away with Baptism, First Communion,

Penance, Confirmation, Matrimony, Holy Orders, or Anointing of the Sick because they don't apply in this day and age, or because we as Catholics walk in perpetual Sanctified Grace? I tell you for most of us it's just the opposite. We should be crawling into Church on our hands and knees begging for another opportunity, a second chance. I didn't crawl into Church but I did get down on my knees and beg for forgiveness. I've been to Confession more in the last couple of years than I had in the past thirty years. I tell you when you begin to purge your soul, you can't stop until it's clean. The good Lord won't let you stop. The Holy Spirit will not move into a dirty, filthy, vile habitat.

Do you know what the sacraments are? According to Christ, they're a ladder plain and simple. Christ gave us a ladder to help us with our journey. They're not a guarantee (you must do your part) but they are definitely the best chance you and I will ever have at attaining eternal life. Each sacrament is another step in the ladder which allows us to reach a higher height. Every step up we take is a step closer to God.

Once you have built your ladder, you can't lay it on the side of the house and forget about it. Consider what could happen to it. The elements can take their toll. Adultery, lying, theft, taking God's name in vain, forgetting about the Sabbath, perhaps putting your faith in something or someone other than God, all take their toll. Your ladder could get stolen by Satan if it's left unattended for too long. How can you protect your ladder? Keep it in the garage (the Church) under constant guard.

While you're in the garage look around, and see if there's anyone else. Maybe you could spend some time in Eucharistic Adoration with the One who's most interested in the safety of your ladder, Christ. You might be there while the custodian (the priest) is giving a tour (Stations of the Cross); if you're really lucky you might be there for an employee meeting (Benediction). Maybe you just need to talk to the custodian one-on-one (Confession). I tell you the garage can be a busy and comforting place if you allow it. I think you'll find the more time you spend there the more you'll want to stay.

I've been to services of other denominations, which I know now was not recommended. I never thought about leaving the

Faith; I always went with someone else. Someone at the man-made church was always trying to get me to convert. There is no comparison. What the denominations call worship, I call Bible study. Don't get me wrong, studying the Bible is good, and we as Catholics have been a little lax on that also, but it's not the Mass. Yes, we have the readings and the homily; a good homily can sometimes change your life. But what is the rest of the Mass? We give praise to Christ! The Mass is supposed to be a re-presentation of Jesus on the Cross, so this makes it a true sacrifice. We worship Christ, that's what our Mass is. We worship Christ and are given the opportunity to partake in the Body and Blood of our Lord Jesus Christ!

I was fortunate enough to attend a Traditional Latin Mass recently. That was so awesome, and the grace in that place had to be record-breaking. The priest said the Mass in Latin, the nuns chanted in Latin, and everyone received Holy Communion at a Communion rail. When it was over, I wondered why the average Mass has to be so watered down!

Our Mass is structured on tradition. The incense, the altar, the offertory, and the sacrifice, it's all straight out of the Old Testament. Read the Old Testament and you'll see the Mass unfold before your eyes. Think about it. The first Catholics were Jewish converts, were they not? Who taught the Jews how to worship? God instructed the Jews on matters of worship. They brought their traditions with them. The way we chant, the way we pray, everything about the Catholic Church is the way it is for a reason.

The Catholic Church and the Mass are not structured for man. The Catholic Church and the Mass were started by Christ. Granted, the Church was launched by Peter, but who instructed Peter? Christ gave specific instructions on how to offer up His Body and Blood. How awesome is that? Why don't we have stadium-style seating like so many of the other denominations so we might be more comfortable? Why do we have to kneel, yet most non-Catholics don't? The same reason, the Catholic Church was started for the main reason of worshipping Christ, the One who will introduce us to His Father. When we kneel we're humbling ourselves before Christ and God the Father. The Mass is not about us, it's about Christ.

The bottom line is this: Christ gave us every tool we need to get to heaven through His Church, but it's up to us to use them properly. The Catholic Church will be here until the end of time simply because it was started by Christ, and is until this day under the direction of the Holy Spirit. Please don't squander away your best opportunity for eternal salvation. Take the first step—a small step if you're afraid of losing your balance. I guarantee you this beyond the shadow of doubt, if you take the first step, Christ will be there to hold you up. Once you reach the point of having an intimate relationship with Jesus Christ you will wonder how you ever existed without Christ as the focal point of your life.

There are so many ways to get closer to Christ. You can read a chapter a day from the Bible and progress from there, or you can take the express lane and begin praying the rosary. The rosary has to be the most powerful tool on the face of the earth. Just let the Recruiter (Blessed Mother) get hold of you, take you by the hand, and personally introduce to her Son. If you want to take it slow you can start with hello, good morning, or maybe I love you, it doesn't matter. Anything you do to show Christ you're thinking about Him will make His day.

His love for us is so deep there is no way to effectively describe His love. Nothing I can write could possibly convey how deep Christ's love is for us. Feeling the depth (as much as I could comprehend) of His love and mercy has forever changed my life. The only way I can describe the depth of His love and mercy for us would be to compare our own ability to love against Christ's capacity for love. If you truly love Christ and God the Father with your whole heart, mind, and soul—I'm talking every fiber of your being—that would be like a drop of rain falling in the Grand Canyon. If our love is the raindrop, Christ's love and mercy for us are comparable to that of the Grand Canyon, which is still a gross understatement of just how deep His love truly is. When I said I couldn't comprehend how deep Christ's love is for us, I meant it. I could definitely feel His love but there was no end to it. I have never in my life experienced anything like it.

As parents we love our children and want what's best for them. As we're looking at our infant children we only have positive thoughts about their future, never considering they can just as easily follow the wrong path. How easy it is for our children to be lured into darkness quite often without even themselves realizing what it is that's happening to them until it's too late. Whether we as parents are made aware of our child's actions through a family friend or the police, one thing is certain: the disappointment and pain is real. The same holds true for Christ whenever we stray. Never forget that Christ died a brutal death on the Cross for all of us. Christ made the ultimate sacrifice for us so we might gain eternal life.

How many of us are willing to go through such pain, humiliation, and torture for our children? Can you better understand Christ's unique perspective and just how much He loves each and every one of us? Our actions may not cause Christ physical pain today, but He most certainly feels the pain of a parent to a greater degree.

Please, from now on consider Christ before acting, and consider His feelings. Remember the bracelets with the letters WWJD (What Would Jesus Do)? Change that to BJC (Because Jesus Cares) and decide from there. "WWJD" never made much sense to me anyway. I for one can't tell you what Jesus would do, but I'm constantly amazed at what He does. To know what Jesus would do is to be able to think like Him and His Father; yet this is impossible for any of us. So much of what we as a society cherish has absolutely no value to God at all. The only thing that matters to Christ and His Father is the salvation of souls. Does God care about our happiness? Of course He does but not at any cost. If our happiness requires us to miss Mass or separates us in any way from the Triune God then we really haven't found true happiness, have we?

Allow me to explore the recent trend of WWJD bracelets for a moment. Let's say you could anticipate what Christ or God would do in any given circumstance. Then it would only be fair to assume that any of us would be able to predict the actions of the Holy Trinity, which also means we would know how They think. If this is true, God has become who and what we want

Him to be; furthermore, we have successfully defined who God is and we're now able to put Him in a nicely wrapped box. In other words, in a strange way God has become submissive to us. Since we know what He'll do, how long would it take before God is okay with everything we do? (Actually there are some so-called Christian faiths that aren't all that far from this belief as it is.)

If there is one constant, if there is one absolute truth, it's God. The truth is that God is who He is. God will never be who or what we want Him to be. God will not change who He is so that we might have a closer relationship with Him. If we desire a closer relationship with God we must approach Him on His terms, through the Father's Son, Jesus Christ. This will require soul-searching (I'm using myself as an example), humility, and Confession—in my case, several Confessions. As I've stated elsewhere in this book, once you begin to establish a truly sincere relationship with Christ, He will purge your soul for you. The Holy Spirit will not take up residence in a condemned soul; rather, a good house cleaning and remodeling is in order and Jesus Christ is just the One for the job.

If we're all in agreement about God and not being even remotely capable of anticipating anything He might do, let's take it a step further. This is something I can't comprehend and also something which I'll likely catch a lot of flak for saying. If we're not capable of changing God into who or what we want Him to be, why are there 33,000+ different versions of Christian denominations? Christ has shown me in no uncertain terms that the Catholic Church is His church. He has shown me that what the Catholic Church professes is the truth. This is also why the Catholic Church cannot change to get with the times. The Holy Trinity is now and always will be who They are forevermore, and it is for this reason the Catholic Church will also profess the same truth from now until the end of time.

Chapter Ten

THE ROSARY

I was raised in the Catholic Church; I attended Catholic school through the tenth grade with the exception of my seventh-grade year. During that whole time I don't remember ever praying the rosary. I would hope I did say the rosary but I certainly don't remember if I did. In fact the road to the rosary was somewhat inspired.

A couple years after I began reading the Bible I also had a desire—a need—to learn more about my Faith. Whenever the opportunity presented itself I would surf the Internet, usually beginning with the word "Catholic" and venture forth from there. The Internet puts a world of information at your fingertips. Is all of it reliable? No. In fact I would argue, depending on which subject you study, you may just as easily find erroneous information. Believe me, there is a lot of erroneous information out there regarding the Catholic Church, but there is also credible information. You can find so much. Excerpts from books written by members of the clergy, biblical scholars—you name it, it's out there.

I visited a website that I know I couldn't find again in a million years. As I was navigating through the site I read a comment that stated all Catholics pray the rosary. I began to reflect on the Catholics that I knew and couldn't think of any who prayed the rosary on a regular basis, if at all. I desperately wanted to learn more about my Faith and I really yearned to be a better Catholic. I decided I would start praying the rosary as often as I could. But as is usually the case, nothing is as easy as it appears. The rosary isn't simply the Apostle's Creed, Our Fathers, Hail Marys, and a Glory Be or two. Oh no, there are several more prayers and mysteries too.

After typing "rosary" into a search engine, I embarked on yet another excursion into the Catholic Faith. The rosary is one powerful tool for prayer. Think about it: You invoke the help of God the Father, Christ, the Holy Spirit, and the Blessed Mother. Get this: the rosary can be used for more than the traditional prayers! Try praying the Chaplet of the Divine Mercy, WOW! I suppose I could explain how the rosary is prayed in both circumstances, but I won't. For those of you who don't know, look it up, and take an excursion into the Faith.

I'm not trying to be rude but I truly believe the route you take back to the Catholic Faith is laid out by the Blessed Mother, the Holy Spirit, or Jesus Christ Himself. If you take an interest in them they will return the favor. I have no doubt my path to the rosary and ultimately the relationship I enjoy with Christ is the work of the Holy Spirit and the Blessed Mother, or as I like to refer to her, the Recruiter.

Once I began praying the rosary I found I couldn't stop. I went from trying to pray the rosary when I had the time to praying the rosary every night. I went from praying the rosary in bed to humbling myself before God, getting on my knees, and praying the rosary like my life depended on it. Believe me, my praying the rosary isn't a habitual thing, for me it's a necessity. I truly don't think I can function without it. I don't remember how long it was after I began praying the rosary to the time I met Christ, but it didn't seem that long a period of time. It became obvious to me that the Blessed Mother is the recruiter. I'm quite sure it was the Blessed Mother who personally introduced me to her Son Jesus Christ.

Whether you're praying the traditional rosary or the Chaplet of the Divine Mercy, either will definitely bring you closer to the Holy Trinity and Mary. I highly recommend both forms of prayer. I know it can be difficult to pray the Chaplet of the Divine Mercy as most people are working at three in the afternoon, a special time to pray the Chaplet since it is considered the "Mercy hour" when Jesus died on the Cross. Nonetheless, if you ever get the opportunity take advantage of it. I think—I know —you'll discover as I did that once you make a habit of daily prayer your life will change, sometimes dramatically, as mine did.

Before beginning the rosary I say a short prayer and ask Christ to send the Holy Spirit upon me. I always mention to Jesus Christ who or what I'm praying for. Usually a couple times a week I pray for the souls in purgatory. Every other week I pray for our president and all of those in public office. I pray they come to appreciate the sanctity of life. Obviously I pray for my family and friends and those I've met that appear to be less fortunate or struggling. Finally, at least once a week, I try to remember the Church, the clergy and everyone involved with the Catholic Church. I know prayer makes a difference. The power of prayer is nothing short of miraculous. In fact, on more than one occasion I would mention to the Blessed Mother that it would be nice to have a two-way conversation with her or her Son occasionally, and look what happened to me. Those prayers were definitely answered. It's not that I've had a two-way conversation, but Christ has definitely communicated with me.

Here's something else very interesting about the rosary. This is something I didn't know until after the fact, so there was no "placebo effect," if you will. I had an addiction to nicotine (smokeless tobacco) for most of my life. I started using Copenhagen in my sophomore year of high school. Throughout the past thirty years I have been hopelessly addicted to nicotine. I always jokingly said quitting was easy as I myself had quit several times. I guess the longest period of time I had ever abstained was two years. That was a long two years, let me tell you. Not a day went by that I didn't crave tobacco, and I was miserable. I had actually given up on the idea of ever quitting, which was okay with me as tobacco was something I really enjoyed. Of course I justified my actions by reasoning it was the only bad habit I had. I didn't count drinking as a bad habit because I wasn't addicted to alcohol and in my mind there was a difference.

My conscience—and I'm guessing yours as well—will allow me to justify anything as long as it's phrased properly and with conviction. One night I was watching a DVD of a powerful speaking priest. He discussed addictions and then he brought up tobacco. He said, "What moron in this day and age doesn't know tobacco is bad for them." Then he had the nerve to say that tobacco use was a sin. Can you believe that? The priest said tobacco use was a sin and used the Fifth Commandment to back it up. *Thou shall not kill!*

The more I thought about it the more sense it made and the more I realized I was the moron with an ethical problem. That night before I prayed the rosary, I asked for help in quitting tobacco once and for all. As I was looking at the three remaining cans, I promised Christ that once those three cans were gone I would never buy or use tobacco again. Three cans later I quit, that was it, end of story. I haven't even had a craving for tobacco since. I don't even think about it. I used to wonder how on earth I would be able to drive without tobacco, but it turns out it is rather easy.

A couple of months after quitting tobacco, I read somewhere that the rosary was particularly good at helping people overcome addictions. I laughed and looked up toward the sky. This whole time all I had to do was invoke the help of the Blessed Mother and the Holy Trinity and not give it another thought.

A coincidence, one might say? If it is a coincidence, you must admit I've had a lot of them within a relatively short amount of time. Could it have been because tobacco use is a sin that I found it so easy to quit? Could it be because I promised Christ I would never use tobacco again? Could it have been that I asked for help via praying the rosary? It could have been all three combined, and most likely it was. My advice to anyone trying to overcome any obstacle in life is the rosary. I am now a firm believer in the power of prayer, and more importantly the power of the rosary.

Earlier I referred to the Blessed Mother as "the Recruiter" and I meant it. As I've mentioned elsewhere in this book, she knocked me flat on my back but if we were to view what happened in slow motion, I think we would find I was really stopped in my tracks with a deep and sincere love only the Blessed Mother is capable of sharing. In fact let's take a closer look at what left me flat on my back.

Let's start at the beginning, of all places, and see where we end up. Keep in mind I am the one who began praying the rosary and I am also the one who would quite often ask the Blessed Mother to speak to her Son on my behalf. But even before I began praying the rosary I was determined to escape that horrible place I had been for the past thirty-odd years. We already know that when I chose to seek God, much to my dismay I met Satan along the way. So let's pick it up after I scaled the fifteen-foot fence topped with barbed wire, and landed face first in a mud puddle full of beer, whiskey, and the smell of stale tobacco. Let us also imagine when I raised my head out of that rancid concoction, I saw a nice clean Bible on a freshly poured sparkling clean sidewalk with a beautiful wooden rosary laying on top.

I made my way to the sidewalk, picked up the Bible and rosary, and then noticed a park bench situated under a bright light, facing the place I had been for most of my life. I thumbed through the Bible and read a passage here and there as I held tight to the rosary, because I didn't remember how to use it. I spent quite a bit of time reflecting on what had gone on behind that fence; I just couldn't believe I ever found the place appealing.

When I first saw the place it gave the appearance of some enormous mansion that always had fun parties which didn't really hurt anyone, because after all, they were just having fun. I remember it being so easy to get in; in fact, the guard at the gate gave me all kinds of coupons for free drinks, tobacco and pretty much anything I wanted. He even locked my wallet and money in a safe so I didn't have to worry about it. I had a good time. At first it was different, and thankfully these people weren't so tightly wound. Anything and everything was okay. Not only were my new associates not judgmental, they didn't expect anything from me and they let me know not to expect anything from them. That was a little different: There wasn't any give-and-take, it was all take.

The only drawback at the party was this pesky Chihuahua that kept nipping at my ankles. After a while, a long while, I was beginning to lose interest and decided to leave. I began to make my rounds and say good-bye, but no one cared. They wouldn't acknowledge me, and that annoying, useless dog wouldn't even acknowledge me. I headed for the front gate and asked the guard for my personal possessions, but he immediately had me detained. I was brought into a room with one chair which I wasn't allowed to sit in. I could see outside through the window in the courtyard that everyone was having a good time and there were actually quite a few new faces. One thing is for sure, this place really draws a large crowd. I bet I hadn't been gone thirty minutes but I did take a step back, and that's when I began to figure out where I was.

Finally the owner of the property came in, sat in his chair, lit a cigarette, and wanted to know what my problem was. He wanted to know where I got off taking advantage of him. He wondered who I thought I was that I could just waltz into his compound, drink and eat, and do whatever I pleased, then all of sudden deicide that I had had enough, and scurry out like a mangy sewer rat. He informed me that I wasn't going anywhere until I repaid him everything I owed him, at which point he held out his hand. I informed him that the guard had my wallet and all of my money. I asked him to have the guard bring me my wallet and money, then I would pay him what I owed, and we would go our separate ways. No harm no foul. The owner shot back that the guard never takes anyone's wallet and that not only am I an ungrateful thief, I'm also a liar. He continued, saying I could work it off and he would inform me when we were even. He then had one of his assistants show me to my quarters, which was nothing but a bare room which I shared with an untold number of people and then he assigned me my duties. It became my job to cater to the new guests 24 hours a day, seven days a week; this was what my life had been reduced to. I was a slave!

This went on for what seemed to be an eternity and I knew full well the owner never intended to give me my freedom. I knew I had to take my freedom back. One day I had reached my threshold and decided I was leaving. The problem was the fifteen-foot fence and the barbed wire, which I did not notice upon my arrival but once inside, the fence was clearly visible and the mansion quickly became a prison.

I decided to make a break for it as I had nothing to lose and everything to gain. I reasoned that I was already dead inside;

what were they going to do, kill me again? I ran for the fence and started the climb to the top without any regard for the barbed wire whatsoever. The guards latched onto my ankles and tried to pull me down, but if necessary I was prepared to drag them over the fence with me or die trying.

I wasn't going back.

Once I reached the top, I negotiated the barbed wire and fell fifteen feet down into a vile, muddy mess. The guards began laughing at me and told me I would be back; there was nothing else they could do as I was out of the compound.

Now we come to the park bench again. After spending some time on that bench I noticed a bright building about midway up the street, so I figured if anything, there must be a restroom where I could clean up a little, at the very least I could get the mud off of my face. As I walked toward the bright building, I realized I was all alone with nowhere to go and more importantly, no direction.

The bright building was a library which was full of nicely dressed people, people who didn't seem to notice how foul I smelled or how dirty my clothes were. The place was huge; I approached the librarian and asked her if I might use the facilities, adding that once I was finished I would show myself out. She escorted me to the restroom and inquired as to why I was in such a hurry to leave after all I had just arrived. I responded telling her that I was not properly dressed and I felt out of place. She looked at me as if I were crazy and then inquired as to what was wrong with the way I was dressed. I replied that notwithstanding the fact that I've been wearing these same clothes for the past thirty years, I'm covered with mud from head to toe. She wanted to know where the mud was as she couldn't see any, and furthermore no one here can see what you're wearing, because we're not capable of judging by appearances.

After cleaning up and taking a good long look at myself in the mirror, I realized I wasn't the same person who went into that compound. I didn't recognize myself. This was the first time I had seen myself in thirty years because where I had been, there were no mirrors. As I gazed on my reflection in the mirror, I came to the realization of where I had been and why there weren't any mirrors. The compound has no use for them because mirrors could lead to self-reflection, which was not to be encouraged or tolerated.

I had seen all I wanted to see for the day, and at that point all I cared to do was return to that bench and go to sleep.

As I was making my way to the door I noticed a bank of computers. There must have been a hundred of them, and there was one in particular which had such a beautiful screen-saver, the monitor screen kept going from purple to white. It was so simple and uncomplicated and yet so beautiful. As I continued to stare at the monitor, the librarian approached me and asked if anything was wrong. I responded by telling her I was fine and that I was admiring the simple beauty of the screen-saver over there. Again she looked at me as if I was losing my mind. She asked me which screen saver I was referring to.

I pointed and replied, "The one right over there, the only monitor that has a screen saver."

"Sir, none of our computers have screen-savers as we can't afford such a frivolous waste of time. We're severely understaffed and could never justify such nonsense, I assure you." She continued, "Are you going to answer the computer or are you going to walk out on it also?"

I looked at her and wrinkled my forehead. "What do you mean, answer the computer?"

"If you can see it," she answered, "and I cannot, then it's quite obvious the message is for you and not I. Besides if it were for me the screen would be that of a green pasture with white tulips on a bright sunny day."

Again she asked if I had any intention of answering the computer. I said, "Ma'am, all I want to do is go back down the street, lie on the bench, and think."

"What bench is it you are referring to?"

"The one down there," I said with a sigh, "across from the compound under the light."

"Sir, the compound is down there, that is certain, but there is no light and that is certainly no place for a bench."

I answered her. "You may have not noticed it because the sidewalk is freshly poured and the lamp post looked new as well.

She replied, "Why would anyone build a perfectly good sidewalk that leads to such a horrible place, a place that does nothing but steals souls and shatters dreams? That just doesn't make any sense." She walked off, then turned toward me and said, "If I were you I would answer that computer because it won't stay on forever and there is no guarantee it will ever come back on, should it turn off."

What is going on? How can a computer know who I am, or better yet, how could anyone have possibly known that I would be here? Not only did I not know I was going to be here, I'm not even sure where *here* is. I decided to check it out. It's not like I had anything to lose. I sat in front of the computer and without even touching anything, a picture of my new rosary appeared. Each bead on the rosary began to light up in sequence, one after the other. It repeated this same sequence of events five times, and then the screen changed colors. The words *you've been alone for so long* slowly appeared, but then the screen gently faded to nothing and became like the others.

I sat there for a few moments, thinking. I finally got up from the chair and went outside with the intent of going back to that bench, because by this time, I was exhausted. As I turned to head down the street, I noticed the sidewalk was no longer there and the same was true for the light. I could not see anything down the street. I stood in beautiful sunshine and there's nothing but darkness down the street. I remember the first time I ventured down there, it always appeared as if there was a party going on but now it sounds much more like agony and suffering. Why did I ever go down there?

I sat on the steps in front of the library and tried to process what was taking place in my life. I was still alone, yet I was beginning to feel more content, if that makes any sense at all. I now know how to pray the rosary and I was also educated about the mysteries as well as their meaning, all without a single word having been written or spoken.

I looked across the street and noticed four kneelers outside the most immaculate garden I had ever seen. I ventured across the street to the garden and that's when I noticed a gazebo precisely in the middle which looked so peaceful, it would be a perfect place rest and contemplate what it was I needed to do next. The gate which granted entry into the garden was locked; apparently this place isn't open to the public, which seems a little odd but in light of the happenings throughout this day it is beginning to seem absolutely normal.

I walked over to the kneelers and discovered only one was open for use. This place is becoming stranger by the minute, after all how a kneeler can be out of order and if they're unsafe why the city wouldn't either repair them or dispose of them is beyond me. For the life of me I can't figure out where I am or what kind of city this is. The streets are so clean it's as if a car had never drove on them. I will say this, never in my life have I felt this safe or content while at the same time having nowhere to go nor a penny to my name.

I decided to take a closer look at the kneelers and discovered they could only be used for a specific mystery, as the mysteries aren't interchangeable. After all, if the mysteries were to become interchangeable, the events of Christ's time on earth could be altered in such a way that man would be capable of completely changing the meaning of the Passion, and then very soon the events of Christ's life would be open to personal interpretation.

The only operable kneeler was the Sorrowful Mysteries kneeler. I tell you I would much rather pray the Joyful Mysteries, or any of the other mysteries as opposed to the Sorrowful Mysteries. I really did not want to pray the Sorrowful Mysteries but at the same time I couldn't stop myself from heading toward that kneeler. I set my Bible on the arm rest, retrieved my rosary from my pants pocket, and proceeded to kneel down.

Before I began praying the rosary, I asked the Blessed Mother to please intervene and speak to her Son on my behalf, as I was feeling very scared and ashamed of what I had done. After the initial prayers and as I began to reflect on the first mystery, I was suddenly in the garden watching Christ as He prayed to His Father with such intensity. He asked His Father to let the cup pass Him by, if at all possible, but His Father's will be done, not what Christ Himself would prefer.

Christ was praying with such intensity He was actually sweating blood. I couldn't take any more of this and I wanted to stop but I couldn't. As I began the next mystery I was standing in the crowd directly in front of Christ as He was being scourged. He looked into my eyes and through me at the same time. He was in so much pain because of my and everyone else's sins, but not of His own doing. I really wanted to get up and leave but I wasn't able to. There were no restraints and I was free to leave but I couldn't bring myself to get up and walk away. As I began the next mystery, the pain was mixed with humiliation. The soldiers had fashioned a crown out of thorns and placed it on the head of Christ. As the soldier exerted force pushing the crown into place, the thorns pierced the skin and caused Christ to begin bleeding. In a short period of time there were several streams of blood running down the face of Christ. As if this weren't enough, they put a purple cloak on Him and bowed down in front of Christ, all the while mocking Him and spitting on Him. Again Christ looked into my eyes and through me at the same time. Crucifixion isn't enough; they have to torment and torture Him also? As I finished praying the mystery I turned and sat on the kneeler clutching my rosary, weeping bitterly and also feeling nauseous. Why did He allow the soldiers to torture Him? Why? Why? Why? Why did Christ endure all this pain for me, not mankind but *me?* Christ has to know I'm not worth that kind of pain and suffering. He has so much love and mercy in His eyes after everything I've done; I know He knows where I've been.

I betrayed Christ after everything He's done for me, my family, and every single person in this world. Yet I turned my back on Him. Christ gave His life for me and I could care less. All I cared about was my own personal pleasure and my happiness, not that of anyone else's and least of all His. Sin is always linked to selfishness and arrogance, and I can't think of one single sin that doesn't involve selfishness and/or arrogance. I can't fix my past, but I can certainly change my future if Christ is willing to give me another chance, a chance to get it right for once in my life.

With resolve such as I never had before, I once again knelt up and continued to pray the rosary. As I begin the fourth mystery, Christ began carrying His cross for all of humanity and He is having a difficult time. Not only is the road full of holes and the Cross very heavy, but His body is in total shock from the pain, loss of blood, and lack of fluids. He just fell; I need to do something, He just fell! Aren't the soldiers capable of showing any compassion at all? Do they have to be so cruel to Him?

Christ is back on His feet and they're once again putting the Cross on His shoulder. The blood from His scalp is still running down His face in places.

This can't continue much longer.

The Cross just fell in a hole in the road and I can see the pain in Christ's eyes; I should carry the Cross for Him. Oh no, He fell again! That's it, I have to carry the Cross for Him, I owe Him that much at the very least. I can't get near Him, it's like I'm not here and no one has taken notice of me. I stand not a foot from Christ—we're looking at each other—yet there's nothing I can do.

I begin to shout, "Lord, I beg you to let me help You, please let me take the Cross!"

Yet, He won't say anything to me. He just continues to look into my eyes and through me at the same time. Finally, the guards force some other guy to help Christ (out of convenience for themselves I'm sure, because they haven't shown the least little bit of compassion for Christ throughout this entire ordeal). With great apprehension, I begin to pray the fifth and final mystery, which is the Crucifixion and Death of Jesus. I would rather get up and walk away but I can't walk out on Him again. This is worse than anything I ever imagined and the stench in the air is making it difficult to breathe. How can anyone drive a nail that size into someone else's hand and have a smile on their face while they're doing it? Now they're getting His feet ready for the nail. I can't watch this. I hear the hammer striking the nail, and I'm getting nauseous again. No one should have to suffer like this, especially someone completely free of sin. They're raising the Cross and they're working it back and forth to line it up with a hole.

Oh no, oh no, when the Cross cleared the hole, it immediately dropped a few feet and then came to a sudden, brutal stop, mercilessly jolting Christ. Lord, I am so sorry. Breathing is really becoming difficult for Him; the simple act of breathing is really causing Him great pain.

Christ just drew His last breath and said, "*It is finished.*"

His mother witnessed His whole bloody and violent persecution.

After completing the rosary, I once again sat on the kneeler and wept uncontrollably. I have just witnessed the death of Jesus Christ, a death that was brought on by sin. When I was living in the state of sin it was as if I denied Christ ever died for me. My constant disregard for the Commandments, in some strange way, put the hammer in my hand. Living a life of sin with no sense of wrongdoing completely takes advantage of what Christ did for me. Again, total selfishness on my part. All I can do is live for Jesus Christ and His Father for the rest of my life. That will in no way make us even, but nothing I or anyone else does will ever be just compensation for what Christ did for all of humanity. All any of us can do to glorify Christ is to live for Him and try to emulate Him for the duration of our time here on earth.

As I got up to leave I noticed the gate to the garden was open, so I entered the garden and made my way to the gazebo. This place is so beautiful and peaceful, but I don't have the energy to walk any further. I just want to rest on one of those benches for a while and think. I didn't see anyone else around and there were several benches throughout the gazebo, so I decided to lie down. I closed my eyes for a few minutes and listened to the birds, because at this point I am emotionally drained.

I had no sooner closed my eyes than I hear a woman's voice ask me if I would mind if she sat on the bench with me.

"Ma'am," I replied, "normally I wouldn't mind and if it were crowded I would certainly sit up so you might have a place to sit, but you and I are the only two people here and there at least five other benches available."

"What you say is true," she agreed, "we are the only two people here. But if there is another bench please tell me where, so I might also relax and listen to the birds. Struggling to focus after opening my eyes, I didn't see a single bench. So I sat up and invited the lady to sit. Our conversation thus began.

"I'm sorry ma'am," I said apologetically, "please sit down. I could have sworn there were several other benches when I first arrived." I rubbed my eyes and tried to focus.

"Thank you, Eugene, it's so nice to see that you're still a gentleman."

"I'm sorry ma'am, but you must have me confused with someone else because my name isn't Eugene, my name is Dennis."

"No," she countered, "I have the right person and your name is most certainly Eugene, at least the person I knew. If I'm not mistaken, Eugene is the name you chose for yourself at the time of your Confirmation, is it not? Didn't you say you chose the name *Eugene* because it was the name of your grandfather?"

After finally clearing the cobwebs from my mind and regaining my focus, I looked in the direction of the voice and saw the most wholesome woman I have ever seen in my life. There was an aura about her. I immediately stood up, then prostrated myself before her, and began to speak.

"I didn't mean to be disrespectful. Had I known I was speaking to you, Blessed Mother, I wouldn't have been so casual."

"Please don't be afraid of whom I am," Mary said, "and please sit back down. You look so tired."

I replied, "I didn't know this was your garden. I wouldn't have made myself at home had I known."

"Please relax," the Mother of God said to me, "you didn't offend me and besides, this isn't my garden. The place in which we are sitting belongs to you."

"How can a place of such beauty belong to me when I don't even know where I am?"

"I would never deceive you," she assured me, "so what I said must be so. However, let's not worry about that right now; instead, let's talk about you."

"Blessed Mother," I objected, "I'd rather not discuss my past if it's all the same with you. I wouldn't feel right discussing such things with you."

"It must have been pretty bad; you've lost that twinkle in your eyes."

"I never knew I had a twinkle in my eyes."

"You sure did," Mary stated, "especially when you would sing to me."

"Blessed Mother, again I mean no disrespect, but I don't think I ever sang to you, as I'm not much of a singer."

"Eugene, you most certainly did. If you recall your eighth-grade class gathered around my likeness in the garden and placed rose petals at my feet while singing to me. It was so beautiful. I think that may have been the last time I saw you."

I pondered this. "I remember that day; I've always remembered that day. The weather was perfect; we were standing near a bunch of clover that had such a nice aroma, that smell has always reminded me of spring. I don't remember singing but I'll take your word for it, because *Ave Maria* has always been my favorite song."

"You look so worn out and beat up. I don't enjoy seeing you like this. I wish you would have asked for my help sooner."

"Granted, the clothes leave something to be desired, but physically I thought I still looked halfway decent. I was surprised I held up so well, given the places I had been. I'm nervous because I don't know where I'm headed, I don't have a clue where I am, and yet I feel so content. Nothing is making any sense to me."

"Eugene, I'm not referring to your clothes or your outward appearance. I'm referring to something much more important: Your inner being, your soul. That twinkle in your eyes which you had at one time has left, and you lost your innocence."

"I have to agree with you," I replied sadly. "I've never known such misery. What I would give to be able to start over!"

The Mother of God answered this directly. "What's stopping you? If you want to start over, then by all means do it."

I wondered at this for a moment. I finally replied to her, "Blessed Mother, I can't go back to my childhood and start over, plus I have so many memories that I once thought were happy, but now all of a sudden it turns out I'm ashamed to admit quite a bit about my past. You know what I find most appalling about my situation?"

"I have a pretty good idea," the Blessed Virgin stated, "but I would like to hear the words you have to say."

"I was the perfect citizen," I began. "I tried so hard to abide by the law, most of them, anyway. People looked up to me; I have never been a follower, I'm not saying I was a leader but I will say I always went my own way. People would follow me because they respected me and what I had to say. As it turns out, most of what I had to say was wrong because what I said would rarely include any reference at all to your Son, Jesus, or to God the Father. I'm discovering that in reality, nothing can be without them. It just makes no sense how one can be a model citizen and hell-bound at the same time. How can the world be so backwards?"

The Virgin nodded her head slightly and answered, "I would say you have quite a lot to share with others now. Eugene, don't let your past drive your future. Jesus is so happy you're finally here, there is so much that needs to be done, and there is so much you can help with."

"Christ knows I'm here? I mean, I know He knows I'm here, but He's happy about my being here?"

"Of course He is! You'll see for yourself soon enough."

"I don't know if I'm ready to meet Christ. I want to meet Him, please don't misunderstand, it's just that He is so holy and I—well it's just that there are so many others much more worthy."

"Eugene," Mary said, "you speak of that which you don't know or understand. You are *just the person* with whom Jesus wants to speak, so do as He says. I know you will be the best of friends in no time."

I forgot my manners in front of the Mother of God for a moment and expressed my own doubt. "What makes you so sure that I'll even get a chance to meet Him?"

"Eugene, you specifically asked me to speak to Christ on your behalf and I did as you asked. He truly is excited to see you. Don't worry, you'll be just fine. Here He comes now! I can't wait for the two of you to meet." She turned toward the adorable Second Person of the Blessed Trinity. "Son, this is Eugene; Eugene, this is my son, Jesus Christ. Do as He says."

With this the Blessed Mother turned and walked away. She then faded out of sight.

The Lord Jesus Christ began to speak. "Eugene, I have been waiting for you. There is much to do and I am so happy that you finally made it."

I prostrated myself again, then knelt upright to speak, but I remained kneeling in His presence. "I'm so sorry for everything

I did, and I don't have any excuse for the way I lived my life. Please forgive me although I would certainly understand if You choose not to."

"I forgave," Christ said, "after you confessed your sins. The past is no more; however, the future is yet to be determined."

"Whatever you ask of me I will certainly do," I answered Him.

"Let us walk awhile."

"I would enjoy that."

The Lord began speaking as we walked. "You have been given much, and much is now expected of you. Through the Holy Spirit, greater knowledge and understanding has been bestowed upon you, and because of this everything is much clearer for you than for most. Take what you now know to be the truth and compare it with the place you came from. Then tell all who will listen. Many will listen to you because you have been where they are. You were shown the way out and now you must show others the way."

"I will, Lord; I make this promise to You: I promise I will live my life for You from now until my final breath. All I ask is that You never leave me. I no longer fear what You and Your Father can do to me; rather, I fear living without you in my life."

"If you and I are separated, it is not I who left you; I will be the one abandoned."

"I understand," I told Him, "and I won't ever walk out on You again. I wish I would have found this place sooner. The Blessed Mother said this place belonged to me but I know I've never been here."

"She was right in saying this place belongs to you," Christ answered. "This place was here, but for a long time it was over-grown with weeds and in need of repair. The place was closed, and neither Me nor the Holy Spirit could stay here. This place where we are standing and talking is indeed yours; we are standing in the center of your soul."

"The center of my soul? Lord, what about the library and all of the people? Where did they come from? Was that a dream? Better yet, is this a dream?"

"This is no dream. What you are seeing is real. The library is where you were given a great deal of knowledge and understanding. The people in the library were all of the prayers that people prayed for you throughout your life. Prayer never stops working to accomplish good if it is My Father's will."

"What about the computer?" I asked. "How did the computer know where I was?"

"The Holy Spirit gave you a deeper understanding through the image of the monitor," Christ answered me.

"What about the compound? Did that place exist or was that a dream?"

"The compound most certainly existed as it still does. The compound represents the place you came from. You see, it represents the state of sin in which you lived. Entrance to the compound is easy but leaving is much more difficult. You must never go back, Eugene, under any circumstances. Heed my warning."

"Lord, I never want to return, I assure You. There's nothing there I have a need to see, especially the owner and that annoying dog."

"That annoying dog was your conscience; he quit bothering you when you stopped listening."

"Will I ever get my conscience back?"

"Your conscience has returned," Christ replied. "You don't see your conscience because it is once again part of you. It's as if your life is starting over, and I will be with you as long as you stay with Me."

I immediately answered Him, "I will stay with You, this I promise and with Your help I won't ever stray."

"Go in peace, Eugene, for I will always be with you. Never feel frightened or lonely for you know where I am."

"My life belongs to you, Lord, as it is because of You that I am even here. I will do my best to convert as many people as will listen."

With this last statement to Him, Christ put His hand on my shoulder, then turned and walked off, slowly fading out of sight.

Chapter Eleven

How to Attain Humility

As Christians we're all called to emulate Christ. The one trait Christ showed us over and over was humility. The King of the world, the Son of man, the Son of God is the most humble being who ever walked on earth. He is the One who can bring the dead to life, restore sight, and cure any ailment. On the eve of His Passion, Christ prayed so hard He sweat blood, yet yielded to His Father's will. The greatest of all men, God made man, was the most meek and humble.

I found one sure-fire way to attain humility. It doesn't matter if you're a world-class brain surgeon or a highly-paid professional athlete. It doesn't matter if you're the CEO of a major corporation with earnings and stock options in the millions. I have found one way to attain humility that can literally change your life forever: the rosary.

I'm sure some of you are wondering just how the rosary can lead to humility. Well, the rosary is much more than a few select prayers. It involves four different mysteries, one new mystery and three traditional. While I won't tell you about all the mysteries, I will emphasize that the Sorrowful Mysteries will humble anyone blessed with the power of reason. After all, the mysteries are a journey through Christ's life and the Sorrowful Mysteries are the most humbling of them all. These are the hardest for me to pray.

Each of the mysteries has a main title and five subtitles that coincide with the five decades of the rosary, which I'm quite sure you figured out on your own. As you pray each decade, you concentrate on a particular event in Christ's life. The Sorrowful Mysteries are: 1) The Agony in the Garden, 2) The Scourging at the Pillar, 3) The Crowning of Thorns, 4) The Carrying of the Cross, and 5) The Crucifixion. Let's take them one at a time.

The Agony in the Garden

Can you imagine knowing when, where, and how you were going to die? Can you imagine knowing you were going to be beaten unmercifully, ridiculed, and crucified? Can you imagine praying with so much intensity you began to sweat blood? Can you imagine going through all this pain for everyone else's sins? That's exactly what Christ endured so everyone would have an opportunity at eternal life. What great feats have you accomplished in your life that measure up to that?

The Scourging at the Pillar

I can't begin to imagine how painful this must have been. The Romans used something resembling a whip with multiple, sharp barbs at the end, which was designed to inflict maximum pain and damage. Every time Christ was struck His flesh was ripped open. Christ could have given up, but instead He allowed the Scriptures to be fulfilled so we might be saved. People have quit jobs over far less, not to mention those who lose their tempers, myself included.

The Crowning with Thorns

After the scourging, the Romans then fashioned a crown of thorns and placed it on the head of Christ. As they pushed the crown in place, the thorns obviously penetrated the flesh. As if that weren't enough, they dressed Him in a cloak and mocked Him, kneeling down and pretending to pay Him homage—all the while spitting on Him. Once they had their fun, they removed the cloak, which at this point was bonded to the dried blood. Again, more excruciating pain.

Whenever I pray the Sorrowful Mysteries I always thank Christ for what He endured but I also tell Him I'm not worth it. How about you? Do you deserve what He did for you?

THE CARRYING OF THE CROSS

Picture this, if you will. You are carrying a heavy wooden cross, a cross made of rough wood, not sanded smooth. Picture this cross splintering and laying on your shoulder and upper back, rubbing against the wounds that were incurred earlier. Again more pain, and don't forget about the crown of thorns. That's why there is blood running down your face. Did I fail to mention you're walking uphill? Don't think for a minute this is a paved road. You are walking up a rough, unpaved path chock full of potholes. Believe me, you feel each and every hole every time the cross hits you in the back. After falling a few times, the guards finally press a bystander into service because your body is in the first stages of shock and beginning to shut down. You still have a way to go. They don't want this place too close to town. It's full of rats and the stench of death.

Are you beginning to get the picture? Would you be able to sacrifice and give of yourself as Christ did? Can you see how easy it is to find humility if you look in the right place?

THE CRUCIFIXION

Once Christ arrives at the place He is to be crucified, they rip His garments from Him, again opening up the wounds on his back. They lay Him on the Cross and drive a large nail into each of His hands and both feet. Up to this point His back was shredded from the scourging. Twice garments have been ripped from His back, reopening the wounds. Blood is running down His face because of the crown of thorns and now Christ is nailed to the Cross.

How do they raise the Cross? They tie a rope on each end and align the Cross with a hole in the ground. Then they pull on the ropes and raise the Cross. As they're raising it they work it so it falls into the hole. Think about this, the Cross falls into the hole, then comes to a sudden stop. Now, think about everything Christ has been through up until this point and just imagine the pain He felt when His whole body was violently jolted after coming to a complete and brutal stop, all the while only being supported by three large nails.

I can't begin to comprehend the pain Jesus Christ went through for our salvation. I will never be able to repay Him for what He did. I continually ask Christ for the opportunity to serve Him. All I want out of life is to make Christ and His Father proud of me. I want to be a source of great joy for the good Lord, not a source of disappointment. I have humbled myself before God. I humble myself before God several times a day in prayer. I strongly believe that you'll do the same thing if you pray the Sorrowful Mysteries one time. All it takes is one time and you will have begun a dialogue with the Holy Trinity and the Blessed Mother. I dare say, it will be a dialogue that will not only change you, but more than likely save your life.

HIS PASSION NEVER ENDS

It must be said that Christ's Passion has never ended. It most certainly ended for Christ as a real historical event, but for the rest of us His Passion continues until the last day of our natural life. This is very important to understand as it appears most of us forgot the unbelievable sacrifice Christ made so we might have eternal life with God.

Christ did not die once and for all; He in fact died once for all. Allow me to explain the difference. For one to say Christ died once and for all suggests some type of finality. Take, for example, the time Pope John Paul II addressed the issue of ordaining women. He sought to put an end to the discussion once and for all. There is also the time Pope Paul VI addressed the subject of contraception, and he too sought to put an end to any discussion. In both instances the respective popes stated very clearly why such things aren't even conceivable, much less open to discussion.

Christ's Passion is totally different. His brutal death and Resurrection are all-inclusive. Christ suffered and died for everyone: past, present, and future. This means that you and I are part of His Passion, and how we choose to participate will determine where we spend eternity. It doesn't matter if one is Catholic and thus has the true Faith, or is a denominational Christian, Jewish, Muslim, Buddhist, Hindu, Atheist, Agnostic... in the end it doesn't matter. Christ has given us the opportunity and the road map for eternal salvation through His one Catholic Church. Whether or not we choose to believe Him is left to each of us.

Christ on occasion has allowed certain souls to experience His wounds through the Stigmata as a visible reminder of His sacrifice for all humanity. Furthermore, the saints quite often allude to the Passion of Christ and also suggest that meditating on the Passion is a good way to unite one's soul with Christ. Christ allowed me to experience His Passion from afar. The story He told about my reconversion that started in the compound, and then progressed to His Passion, and ultimately ended with my meeting the Blessed Mother and Christ Himself was by far the most unbelievable and humbling experience of my life. When I said it was as if the hammer somehow ended up in my hand, that was Christ drawing a parallel between my sinful past and His Passion. Our sins crucified Christ to the Cross; this is something everyone needs to accept. To deny this is to do so at your own peril.

As further proof, I offer Saint Faustina's experience and the two prominent Divine Mercy prayers that Christ Himself dictated to her.

> *Eternal Father, I offer You the Body and Blood, Soul and Divinity of Your dearly beloved Son, Our Lord Jesus Christ, in atonement for our sins and those of the whole world.*
>
> *For the sake of His sorrowful Passion, have mercy on us and on the whole world.*

I tell you, we're part of the Passion of Christ just as all future generations will be until the end of time. Look around, look at this pathetic world. If Christ were to come back tomorrow and repeat the same words, word-for-word from the Gospels, my bet is He would be crucified again. He would be crucified because there are far too many people that prefer this life over eternity. Why is this? Is it because reality is real and eternity is a concept? I appeal to you to look at it in reverse: Reality is conceptually what we make it, and eternity is not only real but forever. If we could live perfectly healthy lives for 200 years, that still doesn't compare to eternity. Why is it that we're so short-sighted?

Look at your life from behind the scenes as God sees it. Christ through His Church has given us everything we need to make it to heaven, and yet so many of us turn our backs on Him. There is only one way to glorify Christ through His Passion and that is to pick up your own cross and turn your life over to God as He Himself did. The other options are many but aren't quite so appealing as far as Christ is concerned. You have so many choices. You can be one of those who call for His death, or you could be the one who scourges Him at the pillar, or how about placing the crown of thorns on His head…. Just which part of His Passion would you like to be identified with?

I am in no way trying to be condescending. In fact it's quite the opposite. I am calling attention to a very grievous situation that I believe many people either aren't aware of, or for one reason or another, fail to believe. Christ put the hammer in my hands. Actually, that isn't correct: Christ made me aware of the fact that through my actions and my own free will it was as if I was nailing Him to the Cross. Can you imagine if I became aware of that after I had died? I owe Christ my life; He quite literally saved my life. Granted, the Holy Spirit and the Blessed Mother played a very big part in my reconversion, as is confirmed in the story, but Christ literally snatched my soul from the hands of Satan himself. How can I not try to make others aware?

I've told Christ on several occasions if He were to exclude His Passion and erase it from my debt to Him, in fact if He were to erase all of my debt with the exception of the last two years, I still have no possible way to repay Him. Would you like to know how much Christ loves us? He would have died on the Cross for one soul. Keep that in mind when you're deciding which part of the Passion you would like to participate in. I'll say this, His Cross is feather-light compared to the weight of sin. The world would have you believe the exact opposite but I promise you this, I would rather give my life for Christ than return to my former of way life.

The night I felt His love, that night I was immersed in His love, it forever changed me. I could care less about money or anything secular because since my soul has been united with Christ, I have wanted for nothing. Actually, He takes better care of me than I ever did.

Chapter Twelve

LEAVING SECULARISM BEHIND

I had no idea that secular society and I were going to go our separate ways.

We are slowly doing just that, and I must say I have never been happier. You would never guess how much time there is for God in your life once most all of the other distractions are removed. My becoming so devout wasn't anything I planned or even thought of; as a matter of fact, I didn't realize I was here until after the fact.

When I was told by Christ that all we had to do was vote pro-life and God would take care of the rest, my life began to change. Up until that point, a large part of my day was spent listening to conservative talk radio as I was driving. Like most sane people, I'm worried about the direction the United States is headed, and conservative talk radio offers some good ideas on how to save this country. Having said that, the talk shows get very redundant, as almost every talk show host brags about himself being the most informative or the last man standing. They always let us know how they're taking the heat for the rest of us and now they even interview each other on a regular basis. Since I learned that all we as a society (actually, every citizen of every country) have to do is vote pro-life, I have quit listening to talk radio altogether. What a relief that has been.

Somewhere in the process I pretty much gave up television as well. To be honest, ever since television went digital, my reception has been less than good. Unless I'm close to a big city on a clear day, the reception is horrible to non-existent. Yes, I have the special receiver and the whole nine yards, but unless I feel like spending $900 to $1,200 for a satellite system, the reception isn't going to get better. I couldn't think of any shows on TV that were worth that kind of money with the exception of EWTN, which I can occasionally get over the radio at no cost. I just recently learned that EWTN is available 24 hours a day on SIRIUS. This I may do as it is far cheaper than satellite TV.

Reception, of course, isn't the entire reason: the real reason is content. The closer I get to God the less I'm able to tolerate secular programming. I used to enjoy watching *Two and a Half Men*. Granted, it was very sexual but I was willing to forego that because it was funny. All of a sudden I could no longer tolerate the sexual overtone. To me the show went from funny to disgusting. Think about this for a minute: we allow television into our homes and pretty much accept whatever it throws out at us. I mean, if most of the show is decent, a little sex is okay, right? As long as the "gay" couple is nice, it's okay right? Really, all we have to do is tell our kids "it's only TV and not real life" so everything is cool, right?

While I was raising my daughters, there were a lot of shows we didn't watch. I wasn't always popular but I was responsible for their souls, which carried more weight than popular opinion. The majority of the programs on television are tasteless and revolting. Would you like to rid yourself of secular TV? I'll tell you how to do it. Start watching EWTN on a regular basis, let's say for a month. Don't watch anything on secular TV except the news if you choose, and watch what happens. I can almost guarantee you will give up secular TV all together. As you're watching EWTN you'll come to appreciate what is important. When you go back to secular TV, you won't be able to stomach it any longer.

Here's the deal: as a society we have been desensitized to adultery, murder, stealing, lying, and God. We've pretty much lost sight of the Ten Commandments; at the very least, the line has been blurred to the point it's difficult to see. Don't think this is by accident. On the contrary, it's by design. The entertainment industry has been slowly lowering our standards as a nation for quite some time now. How great would it be if Christians as a whole quit watching secular TV? Imagine the possibilities: The networks would have to change their programming and quick. This may sound difficult, but believe me, all it takes is one month for you to get your moral bearing back. Once you're back on solid ground you'll begin to wonder how it was you ever allowed yourself and your family to watch some of the shows that came on in your house. Don't blame yourself or feel guilty, just fix the problem. The moral decay happened so slowly it was hard to notice but it seems as though we as a country went from wholesome family entertainment to soft-porn overnight. Trust me, you and your family will no longer be able to tolerate TV as usual. Think about this, if you cleanse your home and family of the filth that is oozing in through your television, you will also at the same time remove a lot of the peer pressure your teens face on a daily basis.

Peer pressure comes from our peers, correct? If this is the case, why don't we just change our peers? What if your kid's peers become the Holy Trinity, the Blessed Mother, and all of the saints? All of a sudden, the normal teen pressure is reduced to a tolerable level. If you can instill in your children a strong faith in God, everything else becomes so much easier for them to navigate. Do they have to give up their friends and become hermits? No, not at all, although I wouldn't be surprised if they let some of their friends fade into the sunset.

When you have God on your side, when you truly believe that with God all things are possible, life becomes much easier. A strong faith in God will change your life as well as your entire family for the better. I know this sounds easier than it really is. If your children have had little or no exposure to God, you have your work cut out for you, but I tell you this: The Blessed Mother and the Holy Trinity are waiting for you to ask them for help. This I promise you, humble yourself before God and ask for His help, and then watch what happens. Things will begin to happen as God draws you closer to Him. You may not see it at first because it will seem so normal, but one day you'll sit back and begin to reflect on how your faith grew by leaps and bounds. Then you'll smile, look to the heavens with tears of joy in your eyes, and thank God for coming to your rescue. At this point you have something to give your family: your faith.

I learned that prayer is very powerful and very real. I've also learned that any prayer related to the salvation of souls is always answered quickly, and quite often you'll be able to see the positive changes almost immediately. This has been true in my case and I know firsthand that Christ is most interested in the salvation of souls.

If all of a sudden you become interested in the salvation of souls, whether they belong to your family or others, you then have something in common with Christ. Believe me when I tell you this, Christ is most interested in the salvation of souls. I can't state that enough. If you show the slightest interest in the salvation of souls, you have at that point befriended Christ and He will in turn befriend you. It is at this point you too will call Jesus Christ your best friend. You will start talking to Him throughout the day; your prayer life will take priority over everything else. All of a sudden you'll begin to look at things differently, as I do. You will always ask yourself one question before you get involved in anything. The question will be the same every time: how will this help me or someone else attain eternal salvation?

Chapter Thirteen

SATAN

During my travels I've had the benefit of listening to many different Christian as well as Catholic radio stations. While I haven't ever heard Satan being discussed on Catholic radio, I have heard discussions on Christian stations. I would hope Satan has been discussed on Catholic radio and I just haven't had the opportunity to tune in at the appropriate time.

I never heard anything that made any sense. I could tell by the way one particular radio personality was speaking that he never had an interaction with Satan. This is a good thing, believe me, but it can skew one's advice and thinking. I can tell you this, the devil is the ultimate opportunist. You most likely will never know he has you in his grasp until you decide to pursue God. I am assuming that up until the time one has chosen to pursue God, he or she was in no danger of being declared a saint. Just wait until that moment—the moment you decide to get a divorce—the moment you want to divorce Satan. If you're ever going to meet him it's when you decide to part company.

I know from experience Satan really hates to be dropped because you have found something better; because you have found God. One thing is certain: God is good, God is truth, and the only thing God can't do is be deceitful. God always wants what is best for us.

Just the opposite is true when it comes to Satan. I'll explain: When Satan thinks he's in danger of losing your soul the fight is on. For me it was spiritual, very real, and very frightening. As

I've already explained, there was a fight for my soul one night, a very real fight. I never saw him but he was there. I have never been so scared in my entire life. I don't wish that upon anyone and although I didn't actually see him, the experience has had such a profound effect on me. Satan trying to retain possession of my soul was the ultimate experience of being scared straight.

He uses other tactics. Actually as I write this, he continues to use them on me. His favorite tactic by far is to create hardships for you. Prior to my reconversion, money really wasn't an issue as I had money in the bank. I would pay all of my bills at the beginning of the month, and would either lend or give money to whoever asked me for it. Life was good. It seemed life was one big party for me. Several times a week I was in the bar having a good time. Now don't take that the wrong way, going to the bar in and of itself isn't actually bad, going to the bar several times a week and getting staggering drunk among other things, that is bad.

All of that and I've never been an alcoholic. I can honestly say I have never had to have alcohol, probably by the grace of God but nonetheless I have never been addicted to alcohol. Since I decided to pursue God, my finances have taken a nose dive. My luck has gone from excellent to somewhere between nonexistent and horrible. As I've noted in other places in this book, under normal circumstances I would think everything that is happening is a coincidence, but considering everything else that has changed in my life I would say I'm being targeted. I've had some of the most outlandish expenses.

Throughout my trucking career I have never been stranded on the side of the road while driving one of my trucks. When I say "my truck" I mean a truck that I own and maintain. Since my reconversion I had a blowout on a relatively new tire. I had checked the air pressure before taking off, everything was good, but the tire blew anyway. When the tire went, it took the mud flap and bent the mud flap holder. I was stranded on the side of the road for five hours. The bill for the new tire, plus installation, plus drive time, plus a road call fee, was more than $800.

In one year I've replaced four windshields. Previous to that year I only replaced one, and that was because the windshield became so pitted over time it was hard to see at night. On one occasion I saw a pigeon come out from underneath an overpass, fly away from the truck, turn around, and it flew right into the windshield. The windshield spider-webbed from one end to the other. I could hardly see. What made it worse was this happened on a Saturday evening on the east coast, and nothing was open. I had to drive at night so the DOT would have a difficult time spotting the damage. Then I had to have a glass-repair company come out to a shopping center in some small town in the middle of Massachusetts to replace the windshield, costing almost $400.

Then there was the time in Spokane, WA, when after doing laundry I discovered my front bumper was pulled out and twisted down. I canvassed some of the drivers around me and no one had seen anything. The strange thing is the trucks on either side of me never moved. The driver to my right said he saw the truck shaking violently and looked to the other side but that truck hadn't moved. The thing is the damage was on the right side; he saw the truck moving but didn't see anything around it. About a week later in California I woke up one morning and noticed my right windshield wiper was bent, and on another occasion all of the plastic ties that secure the different cables to my mirror were removed while I was in Arizona. I could go on but you get the idea. Satan is trying to get me to change my mind. It won't happen. It can't happen.

One thing I failed to mention was this: I did hear some people discussing Satan on EWTN TV and again they were wrong. It was so obvious they had no clue what they were talking about. I caught the tail end of the program and as they were closing, one of the gentlemen said that if you have God on your side, you can laugh at the devil. I can't tell you how wrong that is on so many levels. First and foremost, Christ was the most humble person on the face of the earth, but He never laughed at the demons. As Christ was removing evil spirits He never once acted arrogant or made light of them and they truly were, and are, His enemy.

As Christians we're called to emulate Christ. We're called to be humble. Don't think that because you believe in God, this gives you the right to pursue arrogance. You will be humbled at some point and He may allow Satan to be the one who teaches you humility.

There is another reason that statement about laughing doesn't make any sense. The last thing you want to do is call attention to yourself as far as Satan is concerned. One thing I've noticed about people who had an interaction with Satan is they have no desire to have another one. Believe me, I have a healthy respect for Satan and what he can do, but he isn't God. I quite often pray to God and ask Him to keep Satan away from me. No arrogance there—fear and common sense, maybe even humility, but definitely not arrogance. Laughing at Satan is like picking a fight. How could anyone conjure up such a stupid thought?

If you ever hear someone referring to Satan almost as an afterthought, be very wary of any advice they try to give. I guarantee you they have not a clue what they're talking about. On the other hand, if you hear someone referring to Satan and at the same time exercising caution, that person is probably a reliable source. Respect for Satan can't be taught; after all, from birth most of us are told how evil he is. I would venture to say a great number of people don't really believe Satan even exists, including those giving advice.

I do feel qualified to give advice when it comes to Satan. My advice is simple: Live a good Christian life. Put all your faith in God. Keep holy the Sabbath, attend Mass during the week whenever you're able, and pray as though your life depends on it. Spend time in front of the Eucharist and make Confession part of your life.

Know that Satan does exist and that he is the ultimate opportunist. Then, put him out of your mind. Don't dwell on him or give him a second thought. People with a past similar to mine have a much greater chance of making his acquaintance than a devout Christian. I would even go further and almost guarantee that if you remain faithful to God, you'll never have to worry about Satan. If by the odd chance you do have an encounter with Satan, put all your faith in God, tell God that you know you're safe as long as you're in His arms, and again pray as if your life depends on it because this time it does. You will be victorious. God will come to your rescue, I can attest to that. Then in all likelihood you will feel compelled, as I do, to spread the word of God and save as many souls as you can.

Having said that, I must say that Satan is one smooth operator. He's also the most famous scapegoat on the face of the earth. At some point we must take responsibility for our own actions. I do think he's behind the "pro-choice" (really, anti-life) movement and I believe he's playing an active role in the scandals throughout the Catholic Church and the various man-made Christian denominations. Don't get me wrong, if you're willing to stray into his neighborhood, he'll receive you with open arms but as far as actually luring you in, I doubt it. We're small potatoes compared to the bigger picture. The bigger picture is the Catholic Church and all Christians: that's where I believe he devotes much of his time.

Like I said, if you choose to venture into his neighborhood he will be more than happy to accommodate you. Don't act as if he had to work for your soul when you willingly handed it over to him. Should you ever decide to part ways with Satan, this is when you may very well meet him. You could have an experience similar to mine; I never knew I was his running buddy until I desired more out of life. You see, he really is the smoothest operator you'll ever meet.

When we stray into Satan's grasp it really is the fruits of his labor, but not as you think. There's more than one way to attack Christianity, and oftentimes we don't even notice it. I'll give you a few examples of where I think Satan has been very effective. When I was a teenager I remember a maintenance worker appearing on TV, appealing to the people to vote against whatever bill was being presented to the state legislature that would allow businesses to remain open on Sunday. The gentleman gave many reasons for not repealing the law but the main two reasons I recall were his desire to spend time with his family and attend church with his family. The bill was passed and the law was repealed.

Up until this point the only businesses that were open were those that specialized in family entertainment. Now, all of a sudden, any business could remain open and they began to do just that. It is my opinion that Christianity was dealt a severe blow once the law was repealed. Because Dad or Mom and sometimes both had to now work on Sunday, church attendance all of a sudden had to take a back seat. As a child being raised in a family in this situation, Sunday slowly becomes another day of the week and a generation or two later, their kids and grandkids may have never seen the inside of a church.

Along the same lines, I'm noticing more and more youth sports leagues having games on Sunday mornings. It looks as if Satan is finishing the job. It wasn't all that long ago that there were no youth sports on Sundays unless it was to complete a tournament on Sunday afternoon. This time, it's presented as family time when it's really destroying the family and nobody involved even sees the danger. Before, the stores and businesses were allowed to remain open for the convenience of the families. Do you see a pattern? Satan will quite often use families, yours and mine, as camouflage while seeking to destroy any relationship we may enjoy with God.

Just as God is consistent, Satan is also consistent, since he tries to imitate God. The devil just goes to great lengths to hide it. If you always remember this one rule, you'll never go wrong. Put another way, you won't be susceptible to Satan's tactics. No matter how good and wholesome something sounds, if it will in anyway cause separation between you and God, it is most likely the work of the evil one. God will never cause separation from Himself; the flip side is Satan will always try to cause separation from God. Should you endeavor to get involved in anything that will cause you to miss Mass on a regular basis? I don't care if it's a good paying job, it can't be from God as this will cause separation.

I don't know if I was destined for hell or if God was showing me where I could end up. It doesn't much matter and in some respects I'm glad I experienced it, once all is said and done, because I have a faith in God that's rock solid. I personally know Jesus Christ and He truly is my Best Friend. My cell phone doesn't have to be charged and the calling plan is free. I can talk to Christ whenever and wherever I choose.

Chapter Fourteen

MY PERSONAL THOUGHTS

PRAYER

I have become a big believer in the power of prayer: the more we pray the better we get. I quite often don't pray for anything in particular. In fact, the more I pray the less I pray for. Sure, if there is a tragedy or natural disaster, I certainly pray for those involved, but quite often I leave it up to God. Before I pray the rosary or the Chaplet of the Divine Mercy, I always state the intention and fairly often I simply say, "Heavenly Father, You know better what to do with these prayers than I, so You use them as You see fit." That makes sense, doesn't it? God knows where prayer will do the most good.

One day I literally told God I would no longer pray for myself as far as wants or needs go. If I ever pray for myself it has to have the end result of helping someone else. I sometimes pray for an idea or clue of how to connect with someone regarding Christ but there's no need to waste a perfectly good rosary on that when I can just come out and ask. I explained my thoughts to Him like this: I reasoned that since I've turned my life over to Him, it seems to be a horrible waste of prayers to pray for myself when He is well aware of what I need. Believe me, after this last year I've seen that God is in control of my life so what's the point of asking or worrying about the outcome. He "has my back," and that's all that matters. God has made me totally dependent on Him, and that in itself is not only miraculous but from my standpoint it's humbling and also very comforting.

As I said before, whenever anyone prays for the salvation of souls the response is sometimes instantaneous and quite often very visible. Prayer concerning the salvation of souls is to God what discovering someone with the same passion for your favorite hobby is to you.

If you really want to change and you really desire God's help, ask Him correctly. Don't ask God to make you a better person, because this more than likely won't work. Whose definition of a better person are you praying for? The answer could be most likely *yours* because you haven't a clue what God considers a better person. Whatever God would do, you might reject because you wouldn't understand what was happening.

If you really desire God's help, do some soul-searching, grab the rosary, or at the very least get down on your knees (humble yourself) and enlist the help of Mary. Ask Mary to intercede on your behalf. I can't stress this enough: Be totally certain you're ready for this because your life is more than likely going to change immensely. Now, ask the Blessed Mother to intercede on your behalf and petition Christ to come to your aid to make you the person *He wants you to be*, and then leave everything to Him and His Father. Instead of you becoming a better person (whoever that might be), you have relinquished total control to God and He will respond. Get ready, there will be many tears shed; you won't need anyone reminding you about Confession because you'll be the first in line. There will be more tears after that, which are good because you are on your way to being the person God always wanted you to be.

Hint: Whenever I pray the rosary I look forward to entering the Sacred Garden, as I refer to it. To me the Sacred Garden is as close as I'll get to heaven while on earth. I'm referring to the medallion in the center of the rosary. For some reason, shortly after I began praying the rosary the Sacred Garden became a meeting place for me and the Blessed Mother. After that, it became a place to meet Christ Himself. I'm not sure how this practice started but I look forward to it throughout the day. Think about it: Whenever you pray the rosary you have the attention of the Blessed Mother and the triune God, so why not enjoy it for all it's worth. I always stop and talk after the opening prayers and then again before the closing prayers. I at least say good-bye at that point. I mention whatever is on my mind or something I need help understanding.

Also you know, the lone beads between the decades are another resting place that I refer to as "rest areas." In between mysteries I sometimes stop and engage in another conversation at the rest area. When I said I would ask the Blessed Mother to intervene on my behalf it was in the Sacred Garden. All my conversations were with the Blessed Mother in the beginning, but then after a while I noticed I was praying to Christ Himself almost exclusively. If I'm exhausted I can pray the rosary in about twenty minutes, but normally it takes me a minimum of 45 minutes and quite a few times I've gone over an hour. Never underestimate the power of the rosary and especially the power of the Sacred Garden.

UNFORTUNATE ENCOUNTER

Some of the clergy, at least as far as I'm concerned, is a more depressing topic. Throughout this whole experience (which thankfully hasn't come to a complete halt) I've been on my own. Christ has always provided me with everything I've asked about (answers regarding questions), and it's almost as if He has said, "All eyes on me." Whenever I've asked Him a question it was answered by Him personally or the next day via EWTN radio or TV, but I have always received an answer. He doesn't respond to me instantaneously. If the response comes from Him, it could be a few days and He never just comes out and says anything point-blank. He definitely has a unique way of speaking but He always sees to it that I understand.

I strayed for a minute because in some ways what I'm about to tell you may have been a test. On New Year's Eve, 2011, I attended Mass in the northeast. This was probably at the height of my spiritual experiences. I really wanted to talk to someone regarding my experiences, so after my Confession I asked Father if I could speak to him after Mass, and he agreed. After his homily I remember thinking that he would understand what I was going through. Nothing could have been further from the truth. To be fair, this is when I thought our sin caused Christ physical pain today, but the priest didn't correct me; he just let me go on. When I told Father about my experiences (my spiritual tour) regarding the sacraments and the catechism being guided by Christ, at that point he began to argue with me. I told the priest I knew beyond the shadow of a doubt that the Eucharist is in fact the Body and Blood of Christ. His response to me was that the Eucharist is a symbol for our benefit because we need symbolism.

I also told Father about my experiences regarding Reconciliation. I explained everything to him. I stated that I knew that he was a conduit for Christ in the context of the sacrament of Reconciliation. Again he disagreed and told me that we as people need to know that we're forgiven but that was the extent of Reconciliation. After that we parted company, neither connecting with the other. As I was walking back to my truck, I began to reflect on what took place that evening and everything I experienced through Christ. I came to the conclusion that what I had been experiencing was of Christ.

That night I said the rosary for the priest. I genuinely felt bad for him because he had no faith in whom and what he was selling. Maybe Christ wanted to see if I would give up and go back to my old ways.

I say I've been on my own because no one from the Church has gotten back to me. I emailed the Diocese of Dallas with no response. I emailed the Passionists and Trinitarians also with no results. I even called the number on the website for the Trinitarians and left a message, again no results. I actually walked into the offices of the Diocese of Fort Worth, Texas, and spoke with the assistant to the priest in charge of vocations. Everything went well but again nothing happened. To be fair, the priest was out ill due to stress, which I completely understand, but I did call back a month or so later and again got no response.

Granted, authorities in the Church would rather put a younger person through the seminary than someone my age (fifty). I'm sure they figure I'll no sooner finish the seminary than head straight for the retirement home, who knows. It would have been nice if someone got back to me. I could have used some help in the discernment process but that is neither here nor there, because in the end I don't blame any of the religious orders or the dioceses. I really believe Christ was seeing to it that I focused on Him.

After almost a year of this, I had a few questions. I'm not complaining in the least; this has by far been the best year of my life. I knew everything I experienced was real and I also knew it was Christ guiding the process, but there was a little piece of me that wondered if I was going crazy. One afternoon before I prayed the Chaplet of the Divine Mercy, I asked the Lord if He could put my mind at ease. This was particularly hard because I didn't for a minute want Christ to think I was having doubts, but I explained to Him that I found the whole experience so incredible, I just wanted to make sure what I was experiencing was real, and not my imagination.

That evening as I was driving through Wisconsin, there was a program on EWTN—the name of which escapes me—but they were talking about spiritualism and discernment. The guest was a Jesuit priest whose expertise, among other things, was spiritualism and discernment. As he spoke, I knew the answers to the questions that came up and could have finished most of his sentences simply because of what I've experienced over the last year. Again my prayers were answered. I tried to call in, but the show was a repeat from earlier in the afternoon so the phone just went dead. This was par for the course; however, I did get the email address for the show and considered sending an email with the hope of getting in touch with the priest. After thinking about it, I decided to trust Christ. I mean, He literally answered every question I had through the radio show the same day I asked Him.

JINGLE BELLS?

The Christmas of 2010 was by far the best Christmas I ever experienced. I didn't receive one single material gift, but I gained everything through my intimate relationship with Christ. I was able to attend Mass every day with the exception of one, and I made it to adoration twice. The only downside was when I went to adoration during the Spanish Christmas liturgy, and that was not a happy experience.

Notwithstanding how hard it is to concentrate on Christ when the liturgy is going on, it's even worse when the choir sings *Jingle Bells* during Communion. I looked at Christ and apologized profusely as my eyes began to tear up. If I were the priest, I would have ended Mass right then. I would tell everyone that Mass would resume from the beginning in thirty minutes, and this time we'll worship Jesus Christ, leaving the secular trash outside. On the lighter side, the only thing I asked for was given to me. I asked my oldest daughter, as a gift to me, that she would go to Confession and she gladly gave me what I asked for.

The Depth of the Catholic Faith

As I've been given the grand tour of the Catholic Church by Christ Himself, I have to wonder if any one person can possibly know everything there is to know about the Catholic Faith. This seems like a daunting task—a lifelong pursuit at the very least. The deeper you dig the more there is to learn, and the more you learn the more there is. I'm quite sure there are those who completely comprehend the Catholic Faith and I'm quite sure Pope Benedict XVI is one of them. It is my estimation that this is a very elite group. Just as reading the Bible constantly reveals new and deeper meaning regardless of how many times we read it, the same is true with the Catholic Faith. I guess that's why it's so easy to find fault with the Catholic Church because no one on the outside truly understands. If they understood, they themselves would become Catholic. For that matter, if Catholics would invest some time in learning their Faith, attendance at Mass and in the confessional would sky rocket.

The Sacraments

We as Catholics are so blessed with all the sacraments that we quite literally have no excuse for not taking advantage of them. We certainly have no excuse for living in a state of sin. Do you realize that if we truly lived our Faith, there would eventually be only one Faith for this reason alone? As with the first thousand years of Christian history, there will eventually again only be one Christian faith as Christ said. Knowing how much emphasis Christ places on the sacraments, isn't it time we as Catholics took our Faith more seriously? Everyone should realize just how important each and every sacrament truly is from the fact that Christ Himself desires everyone to become Catholic for the saving graces available through the sacraments.

While all the sacraments are important, Christ stresses the importance of Holy Communion and Reconciliation. Holy Communion and Reconciliation are so intertwined that in a practical sense you can't possibly live one without the other. To live the sacraments (especially Holy Communion and Reconciliation) is to acknowledge our own shortcomings and humble ourselves before Christ, and then ask for forgiveness. If you truly know you receive the Body and Blood of Christ during Communion, the sacrament of Reconciliation is a must. The grace available through each of these two sacraments is mind boggling.

I find alarming the number of Catholics who, for all practical purposes, quit practicing their faith yet continue to attend Mass regularly. Believe me, I am in no way exonerating myself as I acted in a similar fashion, only worse as compared to most. Are we any different than the Israelites of the Old Testament? How many times did the Israelites veer off course throughout their history? Try reading the Bible and whenever the word *Israelite* appears, insert your name. Read the Passion account in all four gospels and insert your name wherever the words *soldier, Pharisees, Sanhedrin,* or *Jew* appears.

Whoever receives Holy Communion while in a state of sin is for all practical purposes mocking Christ. Take your pick, who would you like to be? Would you like to be the soldier who placed the crown of thorns on the head of Christ? How about one of the soldiers that either spit on Christ or drove the nails into His body? If you're anything like I was, you're probably thinking that your relationship with Christ is just fine and all of that talk about the Eucharist and Confession is a bunch of Catholic mumbo-jumbo. I'm here to tell you that everything the Church professes regarding each and every sacrament is absolutely true. I implore you to live the sacraments and experience the unconditional love of Christ for yourself. Live the sacraments and come to know the peace only the triune God can bestow upon you.

THE CALLING

Throughout my entire life I've always felt I was being called to do something meaningful. The only satisfaction I derived out of life is the relationship my daughters and I share, but other than that I can't really say that I've accomplished anything meaningful.

I've earned really good money in my life but money has never been a motivator for me. For most of my life I have felt extremely lonely. It just seemed as if a piece of the puzzle was missing, which is a big reason I was always looking for the right woman (the woman who doesn't exist). She couldn't exist because it wasn't a woman for whom I searched; come to find out I was looking for God and never knew it. I attended Mass without fail yet never found God, if you can imagine that even being possible. Yet for most of my life it was as if a Chihuahua was constantly nipping at my ankles. My problem was I never listened, so I continued the free fall further into sin.

I am so thankful that when I came crawling back to Christ (through His mother), He gave me another opportunity to serve Him. The bottom line is this: If you think for a millisecond God is calling you, seek the counsel of a spiritual director or at least consult a priest and go from there. It doesn't matter if you're married or single; it doesn't matter if you missed your calling to be a priest or a nun; if God has a desire to use you, He'll make it work regardless. I personally believe if more people would take an interest in learning how to discern, this world would be a completely different place.

They say you have to listen for a very faint and shallow voice to hear the Holy Spirit, which I'm sure is true. In my case, however, He has been loud and clear, and on two occasions it has been Christ Himself. If you are ever approached by Christ or the Holy Spirit, that voice in your inner ear is unmistakable and I guarantee you will spend the rest of your life not only praying for another encounter but praying with an intensity that was before inconceivable.

SAINTS

I have contemplated saints quite extensively and just what it is about them that made them saints. It appears to me if there is one common thread, it is their love of God and the Catholic Faith. I can't think of one saint who ever tried to change Catholic doctrine, not that I am in any way an authority on the subject. It seems to me that saints are a living example of what the doctrine truly is. Most of the saints possessed a unique ability to take doctrine and present it in such a way that made it much easier for the rest of us to understand.

I would say they must have at some point connected with the Holy Spirit or Christ Himself. How else can some of their reflections be explained? No amount of studying could possibly lead to such understanding. In my opinion, and that is really all I'm offering here; saints are in fact the exact place where Sacred Scripture and Sacred Tradition come together in the human soul, which is then outwardly manifested for the benefit of the rest of humanity, through the writings and daily lives of the fortunate caretakers of those particular souls.

IN CONCLUSION

I pray that this book brings back those who have strayed from the church. I also pray that everyone who reads this book finds the Blessed Mother, the Holy Spirit, and ultimately Jesus Christ. I don't think for a minute I'm unique; I'm merely fortunate. For all of the downsides of driving a truck, the isolation has proven to be an asset as far as my spiritual life is concerned.

Make time for God and I promise you within a relatively short period of time you'll probably have to make time for the secular world, if just to pay your bills, as it will begin to take up time you would rather use to converse with God.

Chapter Fifteen

LETTER TO MARY

Dear Blessed Mother,

I thought it might be appropriate to write you a letter so I never forget what you've done for me. Where does one start? How can I possibly recall everything you have done and continue to do for me?

Blessed Mother, I hesitate to relive everything as there is so much pain involved, not due to you, but your Son, since He purged my soul. I have never in my life been in so much pain and felt so useless while at the same time feeling so loved. When Christ first told the story of my conversion, I thought it was a behind-the-scenes look at what went on. I didn't get it at the time (I'm quite sure that doesn't surprise you), but Christ said that's what went on inside my soul. Anyone who reads this book will literally be looking inside my soul. As I look back at the way in which I was drawn to the rosary, it is so beautiful.

I found some website that said all Catholics pray the rosary, and then I was led to another website that explained the mysteries and listed all of the prayers. Sad to say, I had to write everything down because I only remembered the Our Father and the Hail Mary. I didn't know anything about the mysteries; that part was totally new to me. This is something I find amazing. The Holy Spirit not only taught me to pray the rosary but He led me to you. From the beginning I prayed to you and asked for your intercession on my behalf. Reflecting on those discussions we had, I would talk to you as if you were sitting right beside me; I had no clue you were listening.

The Holy Spirit led me to you and you led me to Christ. That is exactly how it's portrayed in this book; I didn't come right out and say it, but the sequence of events is the same. I read a book by Saint Louis de Montfort; he says the same thing but much more eloquently. It makes perfect sense and I have to say this is just one more occasion where I've read something after the fact. Blessed Mother, if I could just once learn something beforehand, my life would be so much easier.

After you introduced me to your Son, our Lord Jesus Christ, I began to pray to Him and pretty much abandoned you and God the Father Almighty. I remember on a couple of occasions I would apologize to you and God the Father, stating that I wasn't intentionally ignoring anyone, but my love for Christ was so great I couldn't imagine praying to anyone else. This was a time of great peace and adventure.

I went from the grasp of Satan to being immersed in the love of Christ. I took me three days before I could function in society after that experience. I didn't turn on the radio or watch TV for six months; I did nothing except pray. As you well know, I can no longer tolerate TV with all the suggestive material, and the radio I pretty much gave up on as well; it's EWTN, the Catholic Channel, or nothing.

So many awesome things happened during the writing of this book. The greatest was the unbelievable intimate moments between Christ and myself. Then all of a sudden my world came to an abrupt halt. I remember telling Christ I wasn't going anywhere regardless of whether He would acknowledge me or not. I could and still can tell when my prayers are received. I know when He's listening and when He turns a deaf ear to me. What a horrible feeling!

On one occasion when I was praying I told Him that I knew He was still with me because that feeling of emptiness I had throughout my entire life hadn't returned, but I also knew He was ignoring me. I told Him it was like I would walk into the room where He was seated but instead of acknowledging me, He would turn away. Things would get better, and then they would get worse than before; up and down.

I once told Him it was like I was in the middle of the ocean and He would throw a life ring with a pinhole in it. It wouldn't matter what I did, I was only able to stay afloat for a certain amount of time, but then I was to be submerged into despair once again. At one point I asked just what it is He expected of me. I told Him I didn't have a clue what was going on. I wanted to know if He expected more from me than His Apostles because the way I saw it, they were actually in His presence for three years, and yet they abandoned Him. Then I said the greatest of the twelve denied you three times before he split the scene and you made him the head of your Church; I really pray you don't expect more from me than the original twelve.

During this time I began reading books about the saints and I saw so many parallels it was unbelievable. I write that to tell you this: I've gotten to know a particular bookstore owner, and on one visit he came up to me and said, "You need to read this." He put the writings of Saint John of the Cross in my hands. That book explained a lot. Mount Carmel was in the rear-view mirror, but the Dark Night was far from over.

Mary, I've been pestering your Son for a spiritual director for more than a year now with no results. I've met an awesome retired bishop who helped me some, but he's so strapped for time I quite often feel as though I'm imposing when I call. I've written to different religious orders, called a couple of dioceses, and even visited one diocesan office, all to no avail. I didn't know anything about spiritual directors before this began either. Saint John of the Cross and Saint Teresa of Avila certainly recommend having a spiritual director, as well as quite a few other saints.

Just recently I emailed someone (his suggestion) regarding spiritual direction and alluded to a few of the consolations I've had, but as is usually the case, that is as far as it went. Then a couple days later I received an email regarding spiritual direction, and I asked Christ in prayer if this was something I should pursue. Again, a week or so later I was in the same bookstore and picked up a book by Saint Louis de Montfort titled *True Devotion to Mary.* My reason for purchasing this book was to learn something about you, because for quite some time I wanted to pray to you but I began to wonder what was proper. I was confused, and after being so close to your Son I really wanted to pursue a relationship with you but I didn't know if this was acceptable. Oh Holy Virgin, how delighted I was to find out that not only is praying through you acceptable, it's to be encouraged!

Saint Louis de Montfort does such a good job explaining everything. How stupid and arrogant I was, not intentionally, but the end result is the same. As I read the book I began to think about just how it was I met Christ. I stated in this book that while you and I never actually spoke, I knew it was you who led me to your Son. I reasoned that I went from asking for your help, to praying to Christ, which made me believe that it was you who led me to your Son.

When Christ tells the story from a spiritual perspective, He elaborates on your role in my conversion. Please accept my apologies for being so arrogant. In the book, Saint Louis says there are several ways to have union with God, but the easiest is through you. He says that not only will you keep the devil away but that Christ prefers souls to approach Him through you. Saint Louis also said that with the other avenues one should have a spiritual director and be prepared for the spiritual Dark Night, but with you the Dark Night is much more subdued. As soon as I read that, I hit my knees and began to pray the rosary.

What a relief! It makes perfect sense; I can't believe how stupid I can be. Saint Louis is right; you are the mother of Christ which makes you the mother of God. Okay, that wasn't a revelation, but having personally experienced the love of God which I couldn't completely comprehend and I will never be capable of explaining, I should have been able to see the connection.

Oh, how holy you are! Oh, how the triune God loves you and exalts you above all the angels and saints. Saint Louis is right and I'm living proof of it. Blessed Mother, your Son, our Lord and Savior, was trying to send me back to you the whole time. Why else would I have felt so strongly about coming back to you?

Christ has given you to His Church for the intercession of all. He takes great pleasure in fulfilling your prayers. You are so close to the Holy Spirit. After all, it was the Holy Spirit who brought you your Son, the only begotten Son of God. When you walked to Elizabeth's house you were the most protected creature ever in the history of mankind. You had to endure the brutal torture and death of your Son. You experienced the highest highs and the lowest lows of anyone, past, present or future.

Oh no, most Holy Mother of God, you are certainly no mere vessel as some claim. If God loves me as much as He has shown me after everything I've done, how much more you must be loved! Why wouldn't I pray to Christ through you? Why wouldn't everyone pray through you? Of course God will hear you first, oh Queen of Heaven.

I kind of strayed for a second, but that first night I prayed through you I was overcome by such peace. This is amazing because I've felt the presence of Christ or the Holy Spirit since that one glorious night, but this is so much deeper. In fact, that night I prayed the Sorrowful Mysteries. I remember because I was not able to meditate for some time. For quite a while, whenever I tried to meditate I had horrible thoughts, so I shied away from meditation, but that night was different. From out of the blue, without my even trying, you told me to take your Son's Cross. I did that and He even leaned on me a time or two. I have no idea what that meant, and I don't know that I want to know, but oh, how beautiful it was. I even commented how much closer I've gotten to the Holy Spirit through you.

To most of us He is somewhat mysterious and elusive at best, but you are closer to the Holy Spirit than any creature, and through you I've gotten closer to Him. I actually better understand the role of the triune God individually, thanks to you. I don't know if what I just said makes any sense, but it seems to make my point.

Blessed Mother, I thank you for everything. There is so much more I could write, but at some point everything becomes superfluous at the least, if not ambiguous. I love you so very much, but I'm afraid I'm not capable of expressing it in a way that conveys my feelings and does you justice. So again I ask you to understand and look past yet another shortcoming.

For the love of Christ,

Eugene

About Leonine Publishers

Leonine Publishers LLC makes fine Catholic literature available to Catholics throughout the English-speaking world. Leonine Publishers offers an innovative "hybrid" approach to book publication that helps authors as well as readers. Please visit our web site at www.leoninepublishers.com to learn more about us. Browse our online bookstore to find more solid Catholic titles to uplift, challenge, and inspire.

Our patron and namesake is Pope Leo XIII, a prudent, yet uncompromising pope during the stormy years at the close of the 19th century. Please join us as we ask his intercession for our family of readers and authors.

Do you have a book inside you? Visit our web site today. Leonine Publishers accepts manuscripts from Catholic authors like you. If your book is selected for publication, you will have an active part in the production process. This insightful book is an example of our growing selection of literature for the busy Catholic reader of the 21st century.

www.leoninepublishers.com